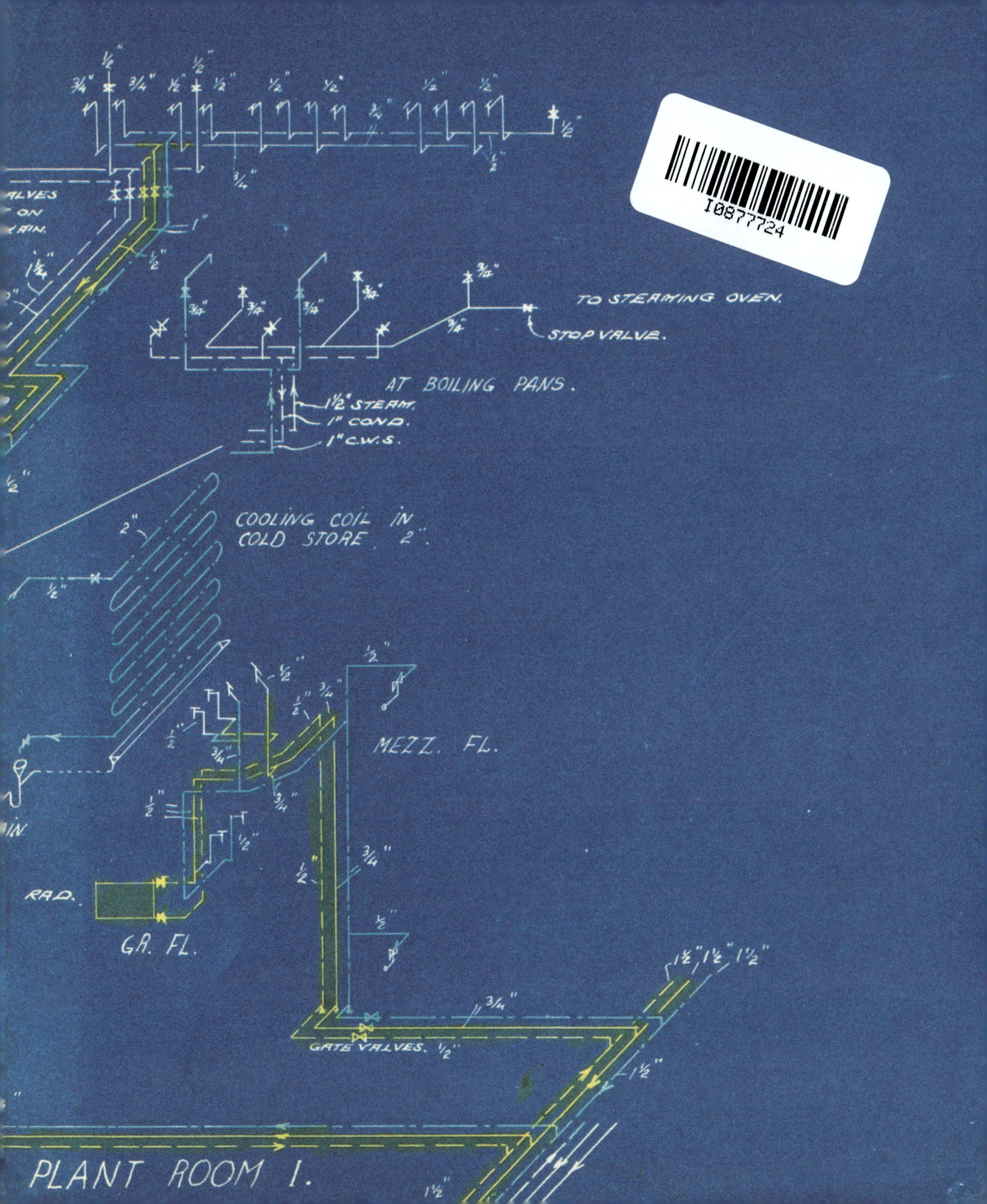
TO STEAMING OVEN.
STOP VALVE.
AT BOILING PANS.
1½" STEAM.
1" COND.
1" C.W.S.
COOLING COIL IN COLD STORE. 2".
MEZZ. FL.
RAD.
GR. FL.
GATE VALVES. ½"
PLANT ROOM 1.

The Dignity of Everyday Life

Celebrating Michael Scott's Busáras

Eoin Ó Broin is a TD for Dublin Mid-West and Sinn Féin's spokesperson on Housing, Local Government and Heritage. He is the author of *Matxinada, Basque Nationalism and Radical Basque Youth Movements* (LRB, 2003), *Sinn Féin and the Politics of Left Republicanism* (Pluto, 2009), *Home: Why Public Housing Is the Answer* (Merrion Press, 2019) and *Defects: Living With the Legacy of the Celtic Tiger* (Merrion Press, 2021). He writes regularly on housing policy issues for a range of newspapers and online publications.

Mal McCann is from Belfast and has been working as a photographer since 1994. He has worked for various local newspapers and joined the *Irish News* in 2007. He has won a number of regional and national photographic awards, most recently the Northern Ireland Press Photographer of the Year 2018 and Regional Press Social Journalist of the Year 2018.

The Dignity of Everyday Life

Celebrating Michael Scott's Busáras

Eoin Ó Broin & **Mal McCann**

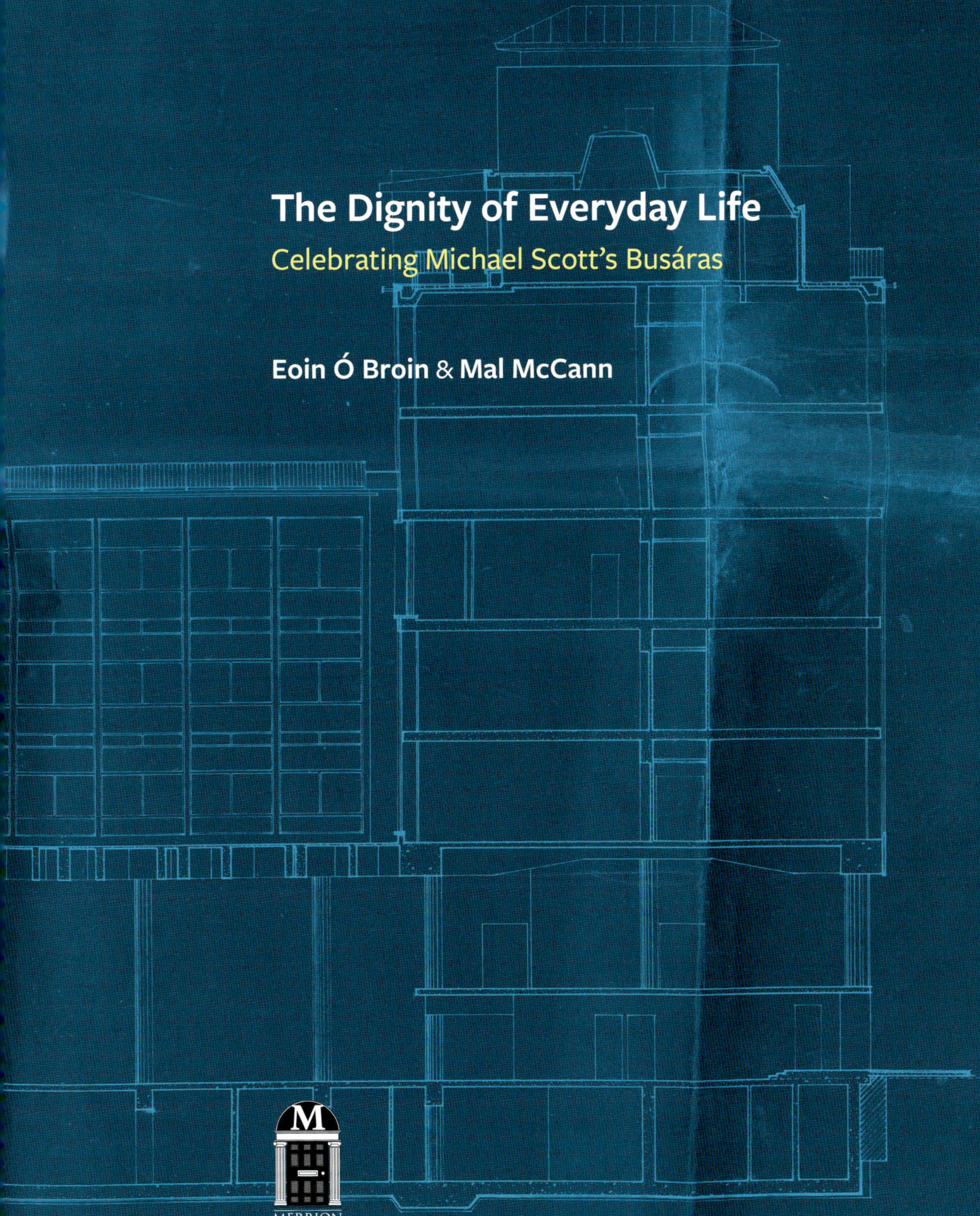

MERRION
PRESS

First published in 2021 by
Merrion Press
10 George's Street
Newbridge
Co. Kildare
Ireland
www.merrionpress.ie

978 1 78537 418 0 (Cloth)
978 1 78537 419 7 (Ebook)

A CIP catalogue record for this book is available from the British Library.

Cover design edit+ www.stuartcoughlan.com
Book design and setting edit+ www.stuartcoughlan.com

Typeset in FreightText Pro and FreightSans Pro

Merrion Press is a member of Publishing Ireland.

Contents

List of Sponsors

Bus Éireann

Department of Social Protection

Irish Architectural Archive

Office of Public Works

Scott Tallon Walker

Acknowledgements

Thanks to
John McKeon and all the staff at the Department of Social Protection, and Adrian O'Loughlin and all the staff at Bus Éireann for their time and assistance with this project, and for their very generous sponsorship.

Niall Scott, Ciarán O'Connor, Lisa Godson and Ellen Rowley for the interviews (and to Lisa for the book title).

Colm O'Riordan and the staff at the Irish Architectural Archive for accessing the Scott archives and giving us their permission to reproduce drawings and photographs.

Ciarán O'Connor and the Office of Public Works for their very generous sponsorship.

Scott Tallon Walker Architects for their very generous sponsorship.

The National College of Art and Design for providing access to their library.

Conor Graham and the incredible team at Merrion Press for all their hard work under exceptionally tight deadlines.

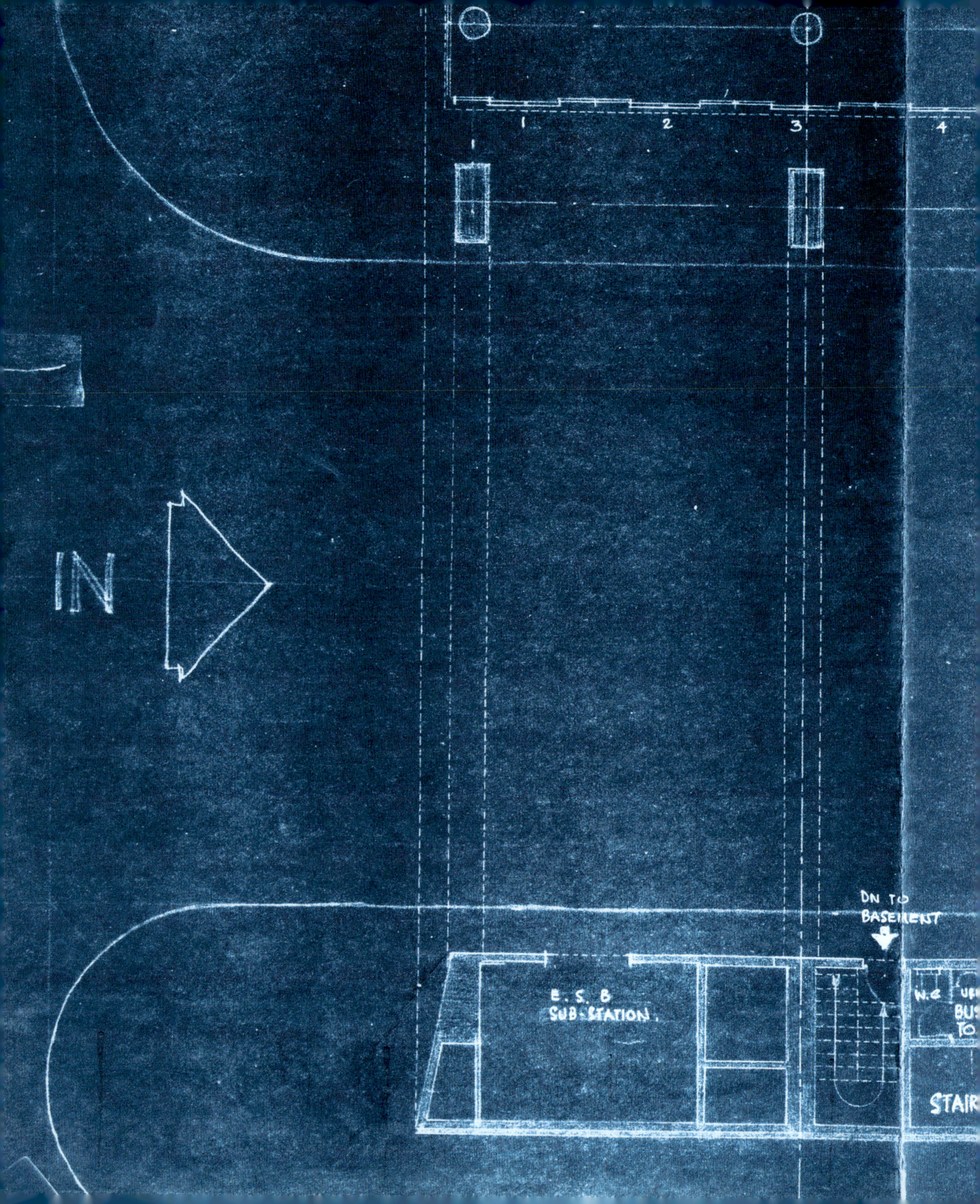
1
2
3
4
IN
DN TO
BASEMENT
E.S.B
SUB-STATION.
W.C
STAIR

Arrival

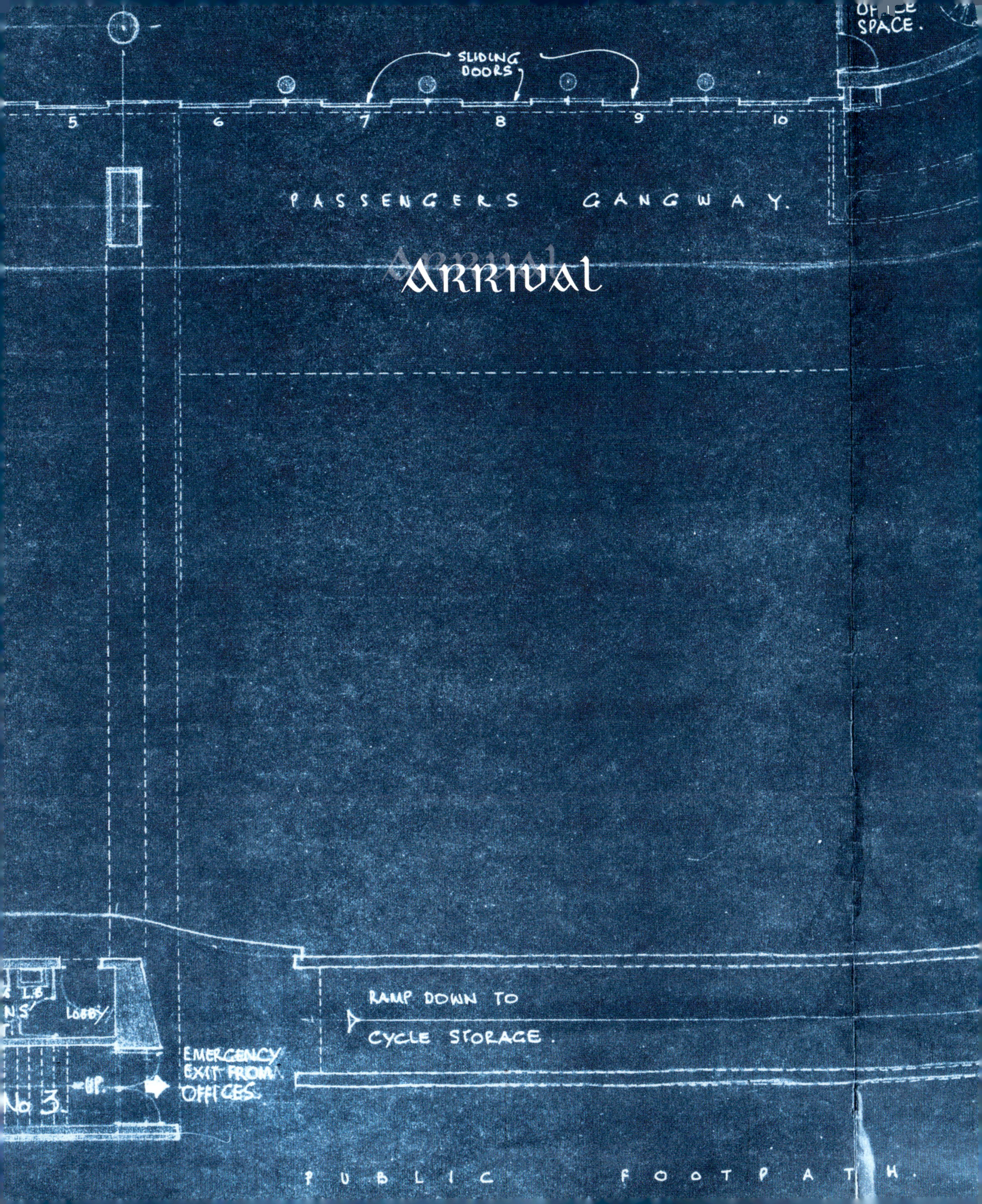
SPACE.
SLIDING DOORS
5
6
7
8
9
10
PASSENGERS GANGWAY.
RAMP DOWN TO
CYCLE STORAGE.
LOBBY
EMERGENCY EXIT FROM OFFICES.
UP.
No 3.
PUBLIC FOOTPATH.

Arrival

An Unseen Building

Busáras is one of those buildings that everyone knows yet rarely looks at. It is a functional building. A building with a very specific purpose.

How many times have you walked past it or through it? Collecting a friend on arrival or getting a bus to the country. Using the basement toilets. Looking down on it as the DART passes overhead on the Loop Line from Connolly to Pearse Street Station.

Dublin's central bus station is a key part of the country's transport infrastructure. Workers, students, tourists, shoppers, hospital patients and day trippers all pass through it in their hundreds of thousands, making their way to and from their destinations. For most people the building remains unseen. It is a place we pass through on our way to somewhere else. Our attention is fixed on what is beyond the station rather than the structure itself.

Landmarks are recognisable features used for navigation. They stand out from their surrounding environment, often visible from afar. Busáras is a landmark, but of a different kind. It is a landmark because of what we use it for rather than what it looks like.

The General Post Office on O'Connell Street. The Ha'penny Bridge over the River Liffey. The Poolbeg chimney stacks. The Central Bank on Dame Street. Cleary's Clock or the Fusiliers' Arch. These are Dublin's standout landmarks. You can't be from Dublin and not know where they are or what they look like. These are the places of rendezvous, of directions, images of our city, recognisable to resident and visitor alike.

But Busáras ... the bus station is different. Yes, we use it for navigation. Yes, it stands out from its surrounds. Yes, it is visible from

afar. But so many of us have an intimacy with the building without really knowing what it looks like.

This is not just my view. The entry on Busáras in the architectural history of Dublin *More Than Concrete Blocks*, tells its readers that 'Many Dubliners walk past it, avoiding it, never looking up and pointedly not engaging with it.'[1]

Part of the reason is its location. It is nestled on a small island between Store Street and Amiens Street. No matter which way you approach it, the building is obscured – hidden almost – despite its imposing frame. From Liberty Hall, the overground Loop Line rail track cuts off your line of sight. From Talbot Bridge, Busáras competes with the Custom House and the International Financial Services Centre (IFSC) for your attention. From Connolly Station, Georgian decay obscures your view.

In the 1980s and early 1990s, the area was bleak and desolate, with little reason to linger. As the Docklands developed, Amiens Street became the boundary between the older, less developed and less populated transport hub of Connolly Station and Busáras, and the emerging high-density, high-income community of the north quays.

Then there's the traffic – Luas, bus and car – forming a moving metal barrier as precarious pedestrian crossings divert your eyes downwards to the road as you rush to catch the last bus to wherever.

But I can't help thinking there is something else at play. Something to do with the relationship between the building itself and the public. Something that can only be fully understood if you know the history of the building. The story of how its original intentions and functions were subverted during the course of its construction, fundamentally changing the relationship between the bus station and the people.

I suspect that, for the majority of people, Busáras is considered a run-down, ugly building to be used rather than enjoyed. But there is a small group of admirers, the present author included, for whom the building is so much more.

Can you imagine Busáras on a Bord Fáilte poster or tourist postcard? Yet this is exactly where the building should be, and indeed once was. Despite our persistent refusal to see it, Busáras is Ireland's most important mid-century modernist building, the history of which has much to reveal about who we are, where we have come from and where we might be going.

Starting to See

I don't remember when I first started to see the building. For eleven years I travelled past or through the bus station while living in Belfast. Was it the red and white candy-striped, mosaic-tiled pillars on the balconies of the third floor? Was it the space-age honeycomb perforated boxes on the roof? Was it the oxidised copper pillars on the south side of the building reflecting the bright green dome of the Custom House? Or was it the wavy, concrete, cantilevered canopy over the bus concourse?

I really don't recall, but something sparked enough of an interest for me to book into the Open House tour organised by the Irish Architecture Foundation in November 2019. That visit changed everything.

To my great surprise, Busáras was part of a much bigger building called Áras Mhic Dhiarmada, the headquarters of the Department of Social Protection. I always knew that the Department and its ministerial offices were in there somewhere, but to my shame I had never noticed the entrance on Store Street.

Nor did I know the building was named after the Leitrim republican Seán MacDermott – member of the Irish Republican Brotherhood Military Council, national organiser for Sinn Féin, signatory of the 1916 Easter Proclamation and one of the sixteen men executed by the British administration after the Rising.

The incredibly beautiful bronze frame for the doors and windows was the first surprise. As was the austere signage in a Colm Ó Lochlainn-style font, almost hidden in deep, dark gold, quietly announcing your arrival at Áras Mhic Dhiarmada.

The door weighed heavily as I pulled the large, organic-shaped Art Deco handle to enter the shallow, yet tall, reception area. A large, bright-coloured tapestry hung above the golden lift doors, which in turn were

Arrival

ENTRANCE
Bus Éireann
Stay safe guidelines
when using
public transport.

separated by deep teak wood panelling. The sensory assault I felt, having just walked in from a dull, grey, Dublin autumn evening, was impactful – but it was only the beginning.

The short tour involved a lift ride to the top of the building to discover what remains my favourite feature, the Pat Scott fin-tail canopy mosaic hanging over the balcony looking down on Store Street.

The remainder of the tour involved a short talk on the history, architecture and design of the building from the rooftop canteen. The deep-red mosaic tiles on the pillars and the almost-gold mosaic tiles in the ceiling skylights gave the otherwise nondescript room a warm glow.

Due to safety works, we could only glance through the windows at the sixth-floor balcony looking out towards the south side of the city and the Irish Sea. The crumbling, multicoloured Pat Scott leaf mosaics underneath each of the protecting canopies were a delight.

It was at this moment I realised there was something very special about Áras Mhic Dhiarmada and Busáras. The building I had grown up around and spent much of my adult life travelling past and through was not the building it was meant to be. This should not have been the first time that I stood looking out onto some of the most breathtaking views of my home city.

The discrepancy between the building that Busáras was meant to be and the building it had become was an intriguing and important story. As I descended the stairs to the ground floor, embossed with radiant green Connemara marble and gracefully railed with iron and oak banisters, I was now firmly committed to knowing the full story of this building.

As I exited back out into the grey November evening, I did something that I had never done before. I walked across towards the Store Street garda station, stopped, turned around and looked at the gable entrance of the building. There for the first time I saw, in its full glory, the main façade of Áras Mhic Dhiarmada – the deep, bronze metalwork, framed with warm, red, Kingscourt brick from County Cavan, on which rested a monumental gable wall of Portland stone, shimmering in the evening light. And, above that, the yellow, red and blue diamonds of Scott's fin-tail canopy mosaic, hanging out over the street below.

How had I never seen this before? Was I always so busy, going to and

from my real destination? Were my eyes so locked on the path in front of me?

For forty years I had walked past something of such incredible beauty and architectural importance and not even known it was there. It had literally been invisible. It was an unseen building. At least now, finally, I could see.

The Dignity of Everyday Life

The multi-layered story of Áras Mhic Dhiarmada and Busáras is truly fascinating. Every aspect of its coming into being was mired in controversy. From the selection of the site, the granting of planning permission and the escalating cost of construction, the building was rarely out of the spotlight.

The fall of the Fianna Fáil government in 1948 saw the building, only just under construction, become a source of high political drama. The new interparty coalition led by Fine Gael was unsure whether to

3009

abandon or amend the project. Heated political debate on the floor of the Dáil and in Dublin City Corporation reflected divided public opinion. Only Fianna Fáil's return to power in 1951 allowed work to resume, though on a much-changed development. Political controversy gave way to arguments on the aesthetics of the building in the letters pages and columns of newspapers, most notably *The Irish Times*.

The new, modern bus station and headquarters of the Department of Social Protection continued to provoke debate and divide opinion. When it finally opened in 1953, bus passengers were at last able to wait in comfort, out of the rain, before embarking on their journey to the provinces. But the public service they now had access to was greatly diminished from what had been originally intended by the building's instigators, Percy Reynolds of Córas Iompair Éireann and architect Michael Scott.

The Central Bus Station, as it was originally conceived by these two men, was to be much more than a bus station. It was to provide its passengers and workers with a range of services and spectacles, as yet unseen in the new Free State. It was to be an expression of the modern Irish nation, in which all people were to be treated with dignity as they went about their daily lives. After buying a bus ticket, passengers were to have access to a rooftop restaurant and balcony in the city's highest building, with spectacular panoramic views from the sea to the mountains.

For those scared of heights and keen to keep up with world events, a twenty-four-hour newsreel cinema was to be located in the basement. In between were to be kiosks, shops, amenities and a second restaurant. This was luxury travel for the masses, for people from all walks of life, travelling to and from all four corners of the country.

And it was to be beautiful, littered with art and design by some of the country's emerging cultural talent.

Reynolds, a veteran of the Easter Rising and War of Independence, was part of that modernising generation of nation builders. He was a friend and supporter of minister and future Taoiseach Seán Lemass, who himself was the bus station's most powerful supporter.

Scott was the country's leading avant-garde architect, heavily

influenced by European modernism, including the work of Bauhaus founder Walter Gropius and Swiss trailblazer Le Corbusier.

Combined, both Scott and Reynolds wanted to give the travelling people of Ireland comfort, convenience and culture. The Central Bus Station was to be a living, breathing expression of modern, republican Ireland, how it treated its people and how it wanted to present itself to the world.

In the end, politics, finance and compromise intervened. The building that opened to the public in 1953 was not a full reflection of its creators' intentions, but much of its original spirit remained. Unfortunately, too much of that spirit remains hidden from public view.

And So, the Book

And so there is value in going back to the start and telling the story of Michael Scott's Busáras. Of course, he is just one of the many names that can rightly lay claim to the building and its legacy. In the pages that follow, you will encounter architects and designers, politicians and civil servants, writers and artists, bus drivers and members of the general public. All of these people played a role in creating the building that stands on the junction of Store Street and Amiens Street today.

The story will also look to the future: that of the building itself, as its custodians seek to invest in its restoration, as well as what the building can tell us about Ireland in the twenty-first century, who we are and who we can choose to be.

The political and cultural battles over Busáras from 1947 to 1953 tell us a lot about that period, including the road not travelled by a young nation struggling to define itself and its place in the world.

Áras Mhic Dhiarmada was built at a time when public architecture mattered, to government ministers and backbench politicians, to public servants in departments and state agencies, and to the wider public.

The lively debate in the columns and letters pages of the contemporary newspapers on the architectural and aesthetic merits of the Central Bus Station stands in stark contrast to the lack of public

T.C.F.I.
IN ÚSÁID
C.C.T.V.
IN OPERATION
COVID-19

response to any major public building project today. In all the recent news coverage of the National Children's Hospital at St James', has the building's design even been mentioned?

In the 1930s and 1940s, public architecture was important. It was a statement of how the nation saw itself and wanted to be seen. And both Reynolds and Scott had very particular ideas about what the architecture, as much as the civic amenity of Busáras, said about the Ireland of its day.

Those ideas, and the debates they provoked, have a relevance to us today. And, in the view of this author, they offer important insights into the choices we have in front of us and where those choices may lead us in the future.

The Dignity of Everyday Life is a celebration of one of the most important modern buildings in Ireland. Much maligned and too often ignored as it has been, we hope that this exploration of the story behind Busáras leaves you with at least some of the excitement that we feel for its history, its architecture, its design, its people and, most importantly, its philosophy.

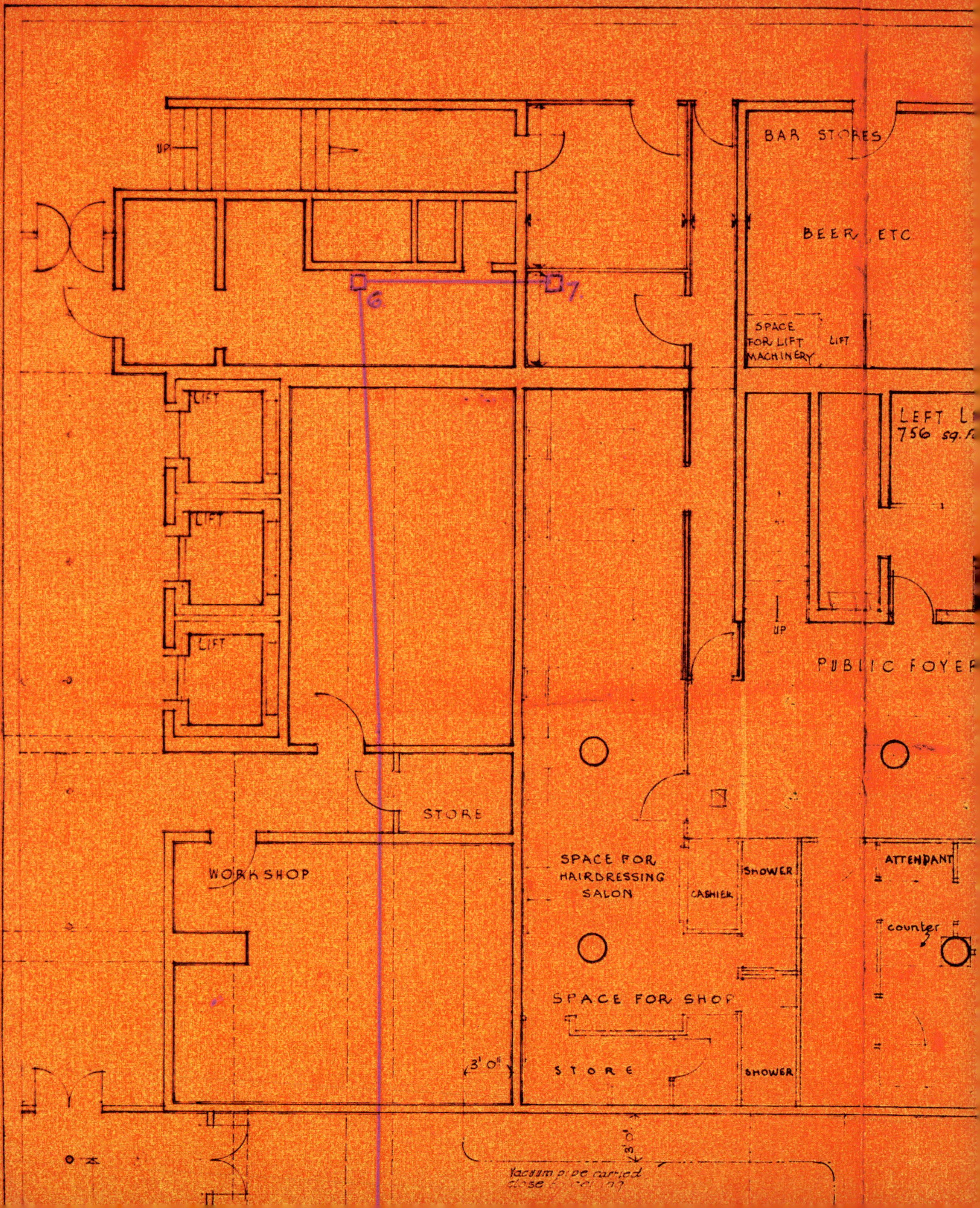

UP
BAR STORES
BEER ETC
SPACE FOR LIFT MACHINERY
LIFT
LIFT
LIFT
LIFT
LEFT L
756 sq. f
UP
PUBLIC FOYER
STORE
WORKSHOP
SPACE FOR HAIRDRESSING SALON
CASHIER
SHOWER
ATTENDANT
counter
SPACE FOR SHOP
STORE
SHOWER
3' 0"
3' 0"
Vacuum pipe carried close to ceiling

History

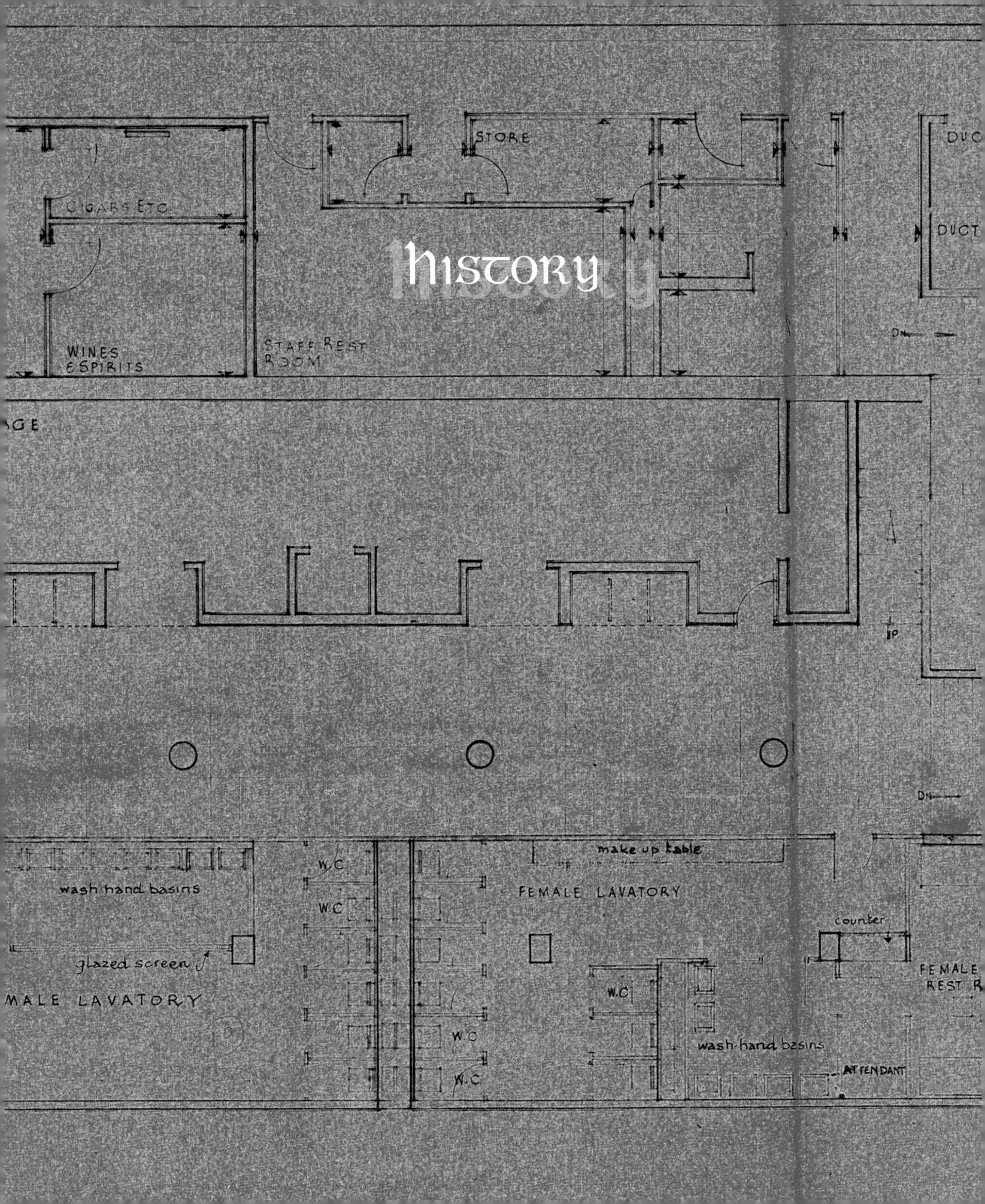
CIGARS ETC.
WINES & SPIRITS
STAFF REST ROOM
STORE
DUCT
DN
UP
DN
make up table
wash hand basins
W.C
FEMALE LAVATORY
glazed screen
counter
MALE LAVATORY
W.C
wash-hand basins
ATTENDANT

History

This great communal work of art, this cathedral to the future, will then shine with the fullness of time into the tiniest things of everyday life.

Bauhaus Manifesto, 1919

The 1940s

Dublin in the 1940s is often characterised as a stagnant and conservative place. Two decades into partial independence, the new Free State was dominated by a heady mix of Catholic social teaching, economic protectionism and nostalgia for a rural Gaelic Ireland long in decline.

Terence Brown's *Ireland: A Social and Cultural History* and Brendan Lynch's *Prodigals and Geniuses* tell the story of this chapter of our history through the eyes of its poets, playwrights and novelists. Brown quotes a line from Patrick Kavanagh's poem 'Lough Derg', 'All Ireland ... froze for want of Europe', as emblematic of the economic and cultural isolation of the time. To reinforce his argument, Brown also quotes novelist and cultural critic Seán Ó Faoláin, who described the 'cultural deficiencies' of the capital: 'The quality of life is weak ... weak for a capital ... Politics, journalism, conversation are generally tawdry, and sometimes far worse.'[1]

Lynch details the poverty and censorship experienced by a generation of writers who were revered abroad but unpublishable at home.[2] Some, such as Behan, Kavanagh and O'Nolan, remained in Ireland, unsuccessfully battling government censorship and alcohol to an early grave. Others, such as Joyce and Beckett, sought inspiration and freedom abroad.

The isolation of the 1930s was compounded by the Emergency, the Free State's neutrality during the Second World War, which further cut off access to ideas and influences from the wider world.

Beyond the literary confines of 'Baggotonia', the political and clerical establishments also had popular culture in their crosshairs. Religious campaigns against jazz, crooning and dancehalls led to the 'devil's music' being banned from state radio in the early 1940s.[3]

Yet, despite all of this, or because of it, the 1940s were also a time of incredible cultural ferment, particularly in Dublin. Ó Faoláin and his War of Independence veteran comrade, the republican socialist and novelist Peadar O'Donnell, founded *The Bell* in 1940. For the next fifteen years, this political and literary magazine was to be the central hub of cultural and social criticism of the Free State's failure to live up to the promise of independence.

Just as writers like Ó Faoláin and O'Donnell challenged the more conservative commentary of mainstream journals, a small but significant cluster of Irish abstract artists – including Mainie Jellett, Evie Hone and Mary Swanzy – emboldened by the return to Ireland of fellow modernists such as Louis le Brocquy and Norah McGuinness, similarly challenged their own vocation's conservative institutions. Jellett and others curated the first Irish Exhibition of Living Art in 1944 in response to the more traditional Royal Hibernian Academy annual show, following the latter's refusal to show the modernist works of le Brocquy.

Avant-garde painting and sculpture were given further impetus as English pacifist émigrés Basil Rákóczi and Kenneth Hall gathered artists with an eclectic mixture of abstract and contemporary styles into the White Stag group. Leading English modernist and art critic Herbert Read was invited to open their Exhibition of Subjective Art in 1944, bringing a touch of surrealism and anarchism to the proceedings.[4]

While literary high modernism, in the persons of Joyce and Beckett, remained abroad during the war, the 1940s would see high modernism in architecture triumph at home. Intriguingly, this flourishing was, in the main, under the patronage of the very government that was censoring an entire generation of poets, playwrights and painters. As the new Free State sought to develop public infrastructure – such as hospitals, homes, technical colleges, power stations and transport hubs – they looked to a new generation of architects offering a more modern style of building.

Throughout the 1930s, local and regional hospitals adopted the austere angles and clean finish of the International Style in Limerick, Portlaoise, New Ross and Tullamore, among other places. Paul Clerkin, in his MA thesis on Michael Scott's Busáras, notes, 'There was a keen interest in architecture from the Government Ministers of the new state …'[5] Key figures, such as Minister for Local Government and Public Health Seán T. O'Kelly, were interested in developments in modern Scandinavian architecture, such as those of the Finnish architect Alvar Aalto, and 'wanted a modern image' in state-funded projects.[6]

The apex of this rush towards the modern was Desmond Fitzgerald's Dublin Airport complex in Collinstown, built between 1937 and 1940, for which he won the Royal Institute of Architects in Ireland Triennial Gold Medal in 1943. The commission came from the state-owned airport. Its design was intended not only to be functional, but also to make a statement about how the then Fianna Fáil government wanted the young Free State to be seen internationally. The building was sharp, crisp, modern and outward-looking. Just the kind of image the government wanted to project to the small number of wealthy visitors who could afford to travel into the country by plane.

But the general public was also able to bask in this new, confident national self-image. State Architect at the Office of Public Works Ciarán O'Connor remembers growing up in Finglas as a child and being taken to the airport on a day trip by his parents.[7] The trip required two bus journeys to see what his mother described as 'a funny-looking building'. Though air travel was well beyond the reach of his working-class family, his mother would drink tea in the modern building and Ciarán would marvel at the modern planes as they took off and landed. Ciarán remembers his mother, who was a staunch Fianna Fáil supporter, taking great pride in the building, a pride in the modern, forward-looking nation that the building expressed.

The Dublin Airport authority were not the only transport agency looking to expand their infrastructure. A newly amalgamated train and

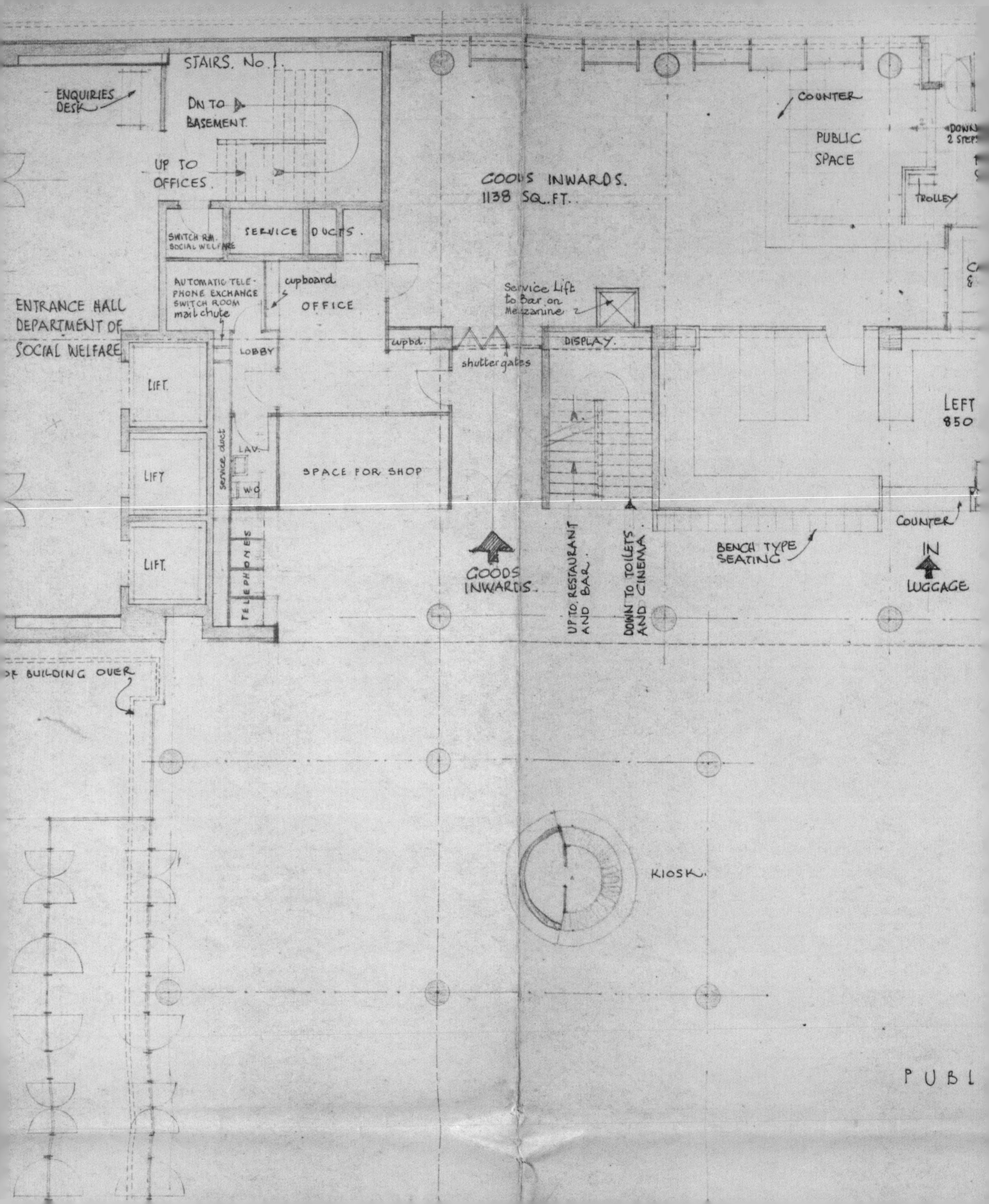

STAIRS. No. 1.
ENQUIRIES DESK
DN TO BASEMENT.
UP TO OFFICES.
SWITCH RM. SOCIAL WELFARE
SERVICE DUCTS.
AUTOMATIC TELEPHONE EXCHANGE SWITCH ROOM
mail chute
cupboard
OFFICE
ENTRANCE HALL DEPARTMENT OF SOCIAL WELFARE
LOBBY
cupbd.
shutter gates
LIFT.
LIFT
LIFT.
service duct
LAV.
W.C
SPACE FOR SHOP
TELEPHONES
GOODS INWARDS. 1138 SQ. FT.
Service Lift to Bar on Mezzanine
DISPLAY.
GOODS INWARDS.
UP TO RESTAURANT AND BAR.
DOWN TO TOILETS AND CINEMA
COUNTER
PUBLIC SPACE
DOWN 2 STEPS
TROLLEY
LEFT 850
COUNTER
BENCH TYPE SEATING
IN
LUGGAGE
OF BUILDING OVER
KIOSK.
PUBL

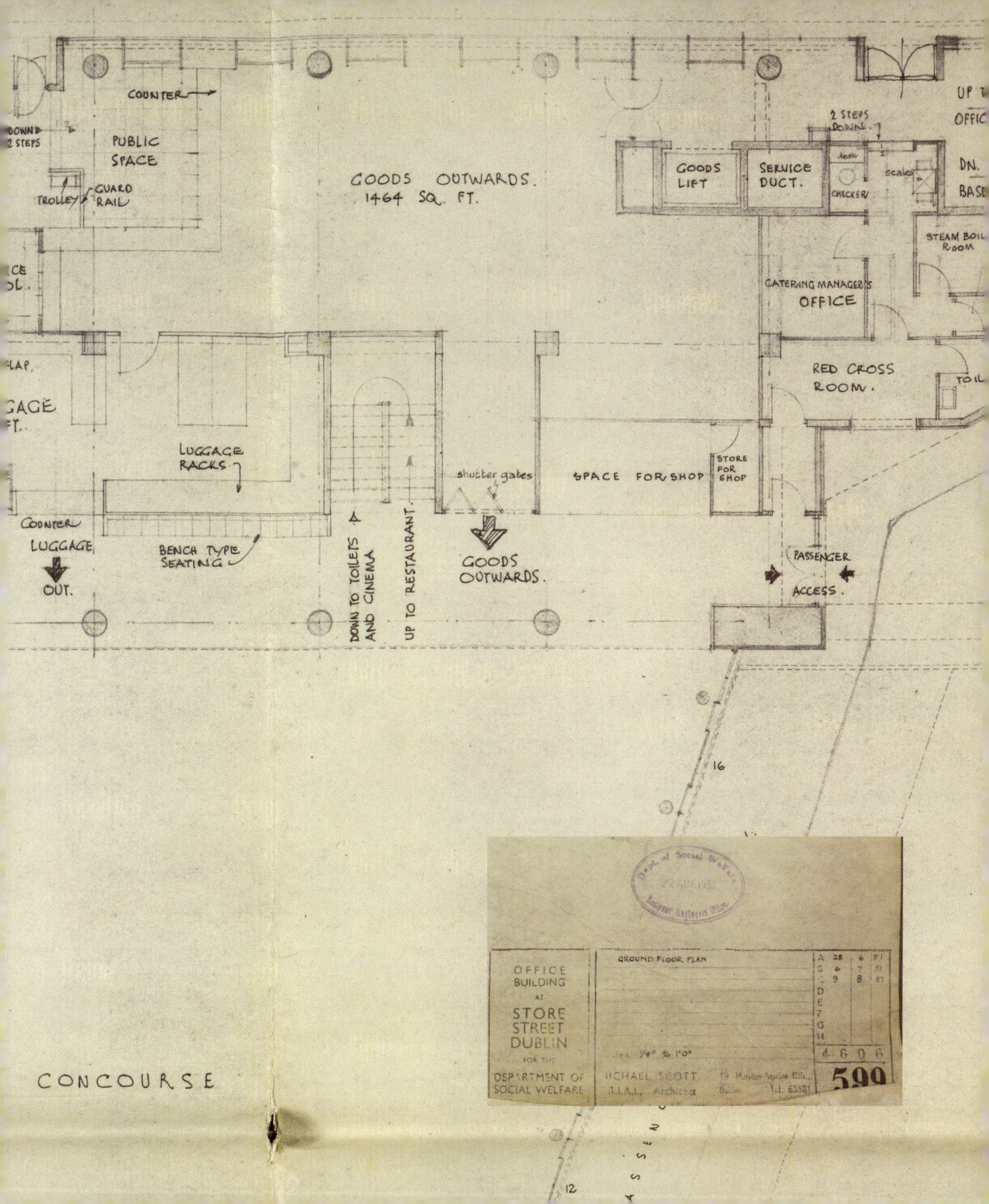
COUNTER
PUBLIC SPACE
DOWN 2 STEPS
GUARD RAIL
TROLLEY
GOODS OUTWARDS. 1464 SQ. FT.
GOODS LIFT
SERVICE DUCT.
2 STEPS DOWN
desk
CHECKER
scales
UP TO OFFICES
DN. TO BASEMENT
STEAM BOILER ROOM
CATERING MANAGER'S OFFICE
RED CROSS ROOM.
LUGGAGE RACKS
shutter gates
SPACE FOR SHOP
STORE FOR SHOP
COUNTER
LUGGAGE OUT.
BENCH TYPE SEATING
DOWN TO TOILETS AND CINEMA
UP TO RESTAURANT
GOODS OUTWARDS.
PASSENGER ACCESS.
16
CONCOURSE
12
Dept. of Social Welfare
OFFICE BUILDING AT STORE STREET DUBLIN FOR THE DEPARTMENT OF SOCIAL WELFARE
GROUND FLOOR PLAN
1/8" to 1'0"
MICHAEL SCOTT R.I.A.I., Architect
4606
599

bus company, the privately owned but publicly funded Córas Iompair Éireann (CIÉ), was about to embark on the most ambitious series of developments, not just in modern Irish history, but anywhere in post-war Europe.

Córas Iompair Éireann

In a time before the motor car, the majority of people in Ireland travelled by bicycle, bus or train. Buses and trains were provided by a series of private companies, including the Dublin United Transport Company (DUTC), Great Southern Railways (GSR) and its counterpart Great Northern Railway (GNR).

The stock was old and in poor shape. Infrastructure, such as bus stations, were non-existent. Passengers would stand in the cold and rain for hours at key pick-up points, such as Custom House Quay on the North Docks.

In 1932, the Road Transport Act required bus operators to apply for licences. The Department of Industry and Commerce would scrutinise the accounts of the companies, regulate their fares and grant the licences.

By 1944, the government had amalgamated the DUTC and GSR into the privately owned but state-funded Córas Iompair Éireann. It would take a further fourteen years before GNR was brought into the fold, by which time CIÉ had been fully nationalised.

In 1945, CIÉ was the largest employer in the state, with 21,000 people on its payroll.[8] The move to greater state control by Minister for Industry and Commerce Seán Lemass was criticised as 'bastard communism' by Fine Gael's Dick Mulcahy.[9] Regardless of the opposition's complaints, Lemass wanted to modernise the provision of public transport and assigned to his War of Independence compatriot, Percy Reynolds, the task of heading up the new transport company.

Reynolds was a 1916 veteran, having fought in the Royal College of Surgeons. For his part in the Rising he was imprisoned, first in Wormwood Scrubs and then in Frongoch, Wales. On his release, he completed his accountancy training and went into business.

In the late 1920s, Reynolds, along with a friend, took a stake in the

General Omnibus Company, buying out the enterprise in 1932.[10] Following a series of mergers, Reynolds took over the reins of the DUTC in 1935.

Reynolds was close to Lemass, sharing the same reforming zeal as the minister. Lemass appointed the former accountant to the board of the newly established Aer Lingus in 1936. When the government forced the merger of the DUTC and GSR in 1944, Reynolds was the obvious choice for Lemass to chair the new enterprise.

Historian Shaun Boylan, in the *Cambridge Dictionary of Irish Biography*, describes 1945 as a positive year for CIÉ: 'the company appeared to have turned a corner, largely due to improved fuel supplies ... branch lines closed since 1942 were reopened [and] in March 1946 Reynolds presented the annual report for 1945, showing a £220,000 surplus'.[11]

It was in this context that Reynolds decided to launch an ambitious investment programme in state-sponsored transport infrastructure. The first phase was to include three major projects in Dublin: a large bus garage at Donnybrook, an industrial-scale chassis factory in Inchicore, and a new Central Bus Station in the city centre. Announced in 1945, this was not just the largest public infrastructure project of its time in Ireland. With the rest of Europe still struggling with the physical devastation of the Second World War, it was reputed to be the largest construction project anywhere on the continent.

The decision by Reynolds to appoint Michael Scott as consultant architect was significant. Together the two men drove a cluster of projects that were groundbreaking in technological, architectural and social terms.

Michael Scott

Born in 1905 in Drogheda to Kerry parents, Scott developed an early interest in the arts. A keen amateur dramatist, on leaving school he attended classes at the Abbey School of Acting and the Metropolitan School of Art. During the 1920s, he acted in a series of plays, including an Abbey Players tour of the United States with Seán O'Casey's *The Plough and the Stars* and *Juno and the Paycock*.

While supportive of his dramatic ambitions, Scott's parents were keen that he had a profession to fall back on. They encouraged him to take up an architectural apprenticeship with Jones and Kelly Architects in Dublin. The practice was described by Scott as 'very mundane', though not unsuccessful, as it won 'two competitions: one for Ballymena Town Hall and [another] for Cork City Hall'.[12]

After working for a time in the Office of Public Works, Scott set up his own practice in 1929. For the next ten years he built up an impressive body of private and public work, including designs for the never-built St Ultan's Children's Hospital modernisation in 1929, two county hospitals in Portlaoise and Tullamore, and a series of Art Deco cinemas for the Ritz chain in Carlow, Athlone and Clonmel.

During this period, Scott became increasingly influenced by developments in European architecture, in particular trends in Holland, Germany and France. A trip to the Netherlands in the early 1930s introduced him to the De Stijl member J.J.P. Oud, responsible for many of Amsterdam's public housing projects in the 1920s and 1930s.

It was also at this time that Scott 'became aware of Frank Lloyd Wright and Le Corbusier, Gropius and the Bauhaus', architects who were to have a lasting influence on his mature work.[13]

Scott's big breakthrough came in 1939, when he was commissioned to design the Irish pavilion at the New York World Fair. Architectural historian Paul Larmour described the significance of the World Fair both for the Free State and for Michael Scott: 'This was Ireland's first appearance as an independent state at an international exposition or fair, and there was, therefore, an opportunity, and a desire on the government's part, to make a statement about national identity with a building of recognisable Irish character.'[14]

The result was a design that was both Irish and international in equal measure. It combined the sleek avant-garde functionalism of Bauhaus design with a display of some of the finest contemporary Irish artists. Sean Keating's mural of the Ardnacrusha hydroelectric power scheme in County Clare, itself a significant modernising achievement of the young state, held pride of place.

As an indication of the success of the project, Michael Scott was made an honorary citizen of New York City, greatly adding to his prestige at home.

Scott's work in the early 1940s was a mixture of private residential homes; public housing, including the Charlemont Street flats; and commercial work, such as O'Rourke's bakery in Dublin. However, it was his appointment as consultant architect for CIÉ by Percy Reynolds that would provide him with his greatest opportunity to date.

Scott's Team

One of Scott's greatest strengths was his ability to spot talent and to give it the space to grow and flourish. While committed to nurturing Irish architects, designers and engineers and using local craftspeople and products, Scott was always looking for the most modern developments in engineering, design and materials. Nowhere was this combination of the domestic and international more in evidence than in the three completed projects for CIÉ.

While the Donnybrook bus garage and Inchicore chassis factory both contained significant innovations in design and construction, it was the Central Bus Station, today known as Busáras, that brought all of these elements together in what is undoubtedly Scott's greatest work.

Like all significant achievements, Busáras was a collective effort. In fact, other than selecting the team and signing off on their work, almost all of the design and detail of the bus station was the work of other members of Scott's team. According to Clerkin, Wilfred Cantwell was 'responsible for the basic design of the building'.[15] Cantwell joined Scott's practice in 1944 and was the appointed project manager on the Busáras project. He was assisted by the 'brilliant draughtsman' Kevin Fox and the equally talented architect Kevin Roche.[16]

Beyond contributing to the design of the main building, Scott also assembled some of the most talented young designers for the details, including Robin Walker, Pat Scott and Barney Heron. Walker designed the furniture, Scott the mosaics and Heron the iron-work banisters and handrails.

For the more complex engineering work Scott looked abroad, recruiting the Danish-born Ove Arup to assist with the use of concrete. Arup and Scott had already built up a significant relationship working on the Donnybrook garage and Inchicore chassis factory. According to Clerkin, Arup's 'practice became known for its fresh approach to difficult structural problems [and] for his new ideas of concrete construction'.[17] This approach is most evident in the corrugated-concrete canopy in Busáras.

However, having a talented team and strong political backing, from both CIÉ chairperson Percy Reynolds as well as Minister for Industry

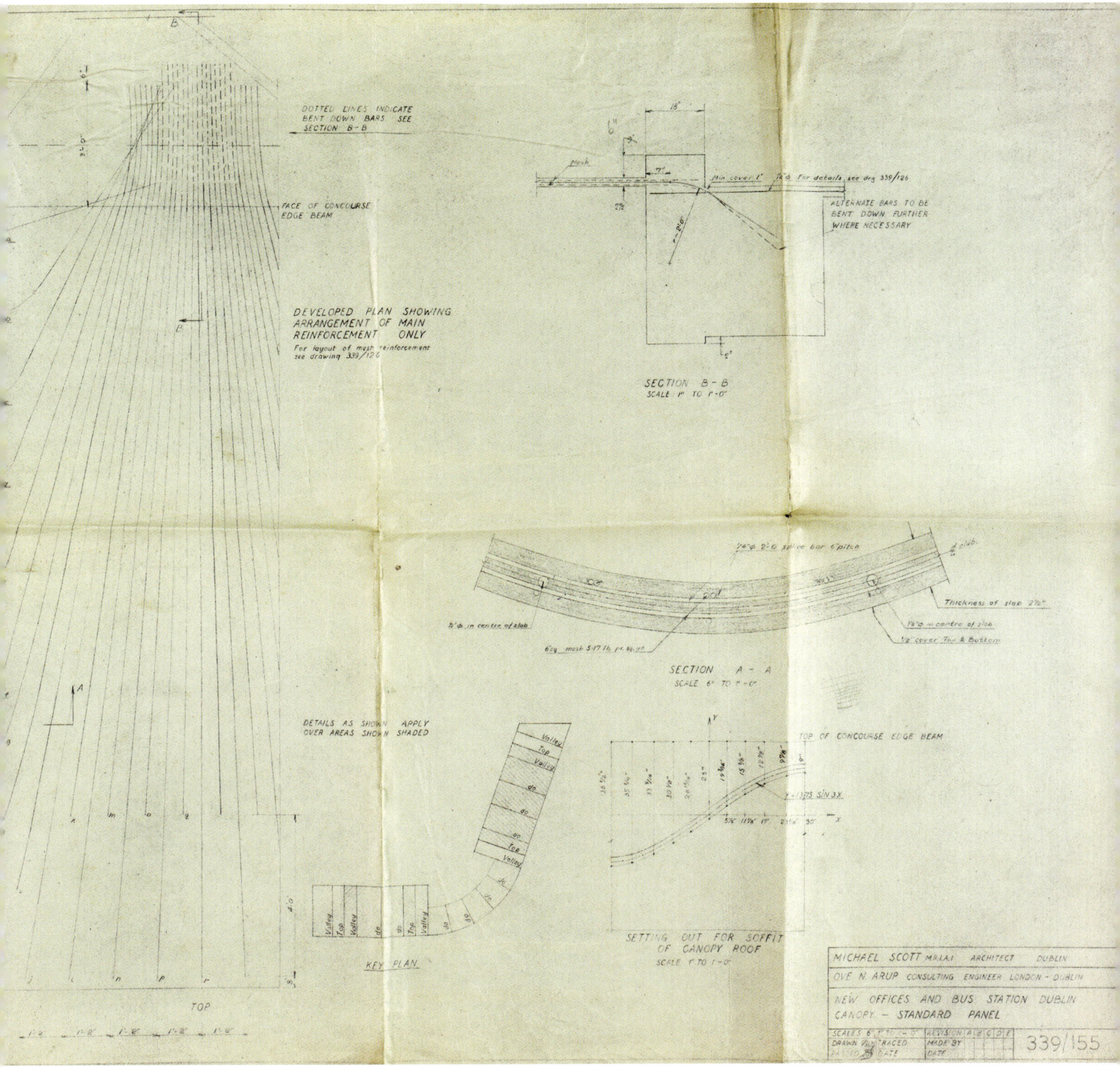
DOTTED LINES INDICATE BENT DOWN BARS SEE SECTION B-B
FACE OF CONCOURSE EDGE BEAM
DEVELOPED PLAN SHOWING ARRANGEMENT OF MAIN REINFORCEMENT ONLY
For layout of mesh reinforcement see drawing 339/126
ALTERNATE BARS TO BE BENT DOWN FURTHER WHERE NECESSARY
SECTION B - B
SCALE 1" TO 1'-0"
Thickness of slab 2½"
SECTION A - A
SCALE 6" TO 1'-0"
DETAILS AS SHOWN APPLY OVER AREAS SHOWN SHADED
TOP OF CONCOURSE EDGE BEAM
KEY PLAN
SETTING OUT FOR SOFFIT OF CANOPY ROOF
TOP
MICHAEL SCOTT M.R.I.A.I ARCHITECT DUBLIN
OVE N. ARUP CONSULTING ENGINEER LONDON - DUBLIN
NEW OFFICES AND BUS STATION DUBLIN
CANOPY - STANDARD PANEL
339/155

and Commerce Seán Lemass, wouldn't protect the Central Bus Station project from problems. Almost every single aspect of the job, from the choice of the site to the design, cost and ultimate use of the building, would become embroiled in controversy during the nine years of the development's life.

Battle over the Site

Plans for a Central Bus Station date as far back as 1922, when the Abercrombie Report proposed Aston Quay as the preferred location. This recommendation, along with the rest of the report's proposals for the reconstruction of Dublin's streetscape, was all but ignored.

During the 1930s, bus passengers were demanding better facilities, including 'the provision of bus shelters along the quays where long distance bus passengers caught their buses'.[18] In 1937, the magazine *Irish Builder* proposed the building of a bus station 'on the bonding warehouse site next to the disused and abandoned Custom House Dock'.[19]

However, two alternative sites were also under consideration: Aston Quay, as originally proposed by Abercrombie, and Wood Quay. Dublin Corporation was in favour of the Wood Quay site, while some in Central Government preferred the Aston Quay location due to its proximity to the city centre.

CIÉ had a strong preference for the Custom House Dock site on Store Street, as it was close to Amiens Street (now Connolly) train station and the North Docks. Siting a major bus depot there would add to this area's position as the city's central transportation hub, including bus, rail and ferry.

Despite the clear difference of opinion between the various players, CIÉ 'went ahead and bought the Store Street site from the Dublin Port and Docks Board for £13,000'.[20] While this appeared to settle the matter, the issue of whether this was the most appropriate site for the Central Bus Station was to re-emerge some years later.

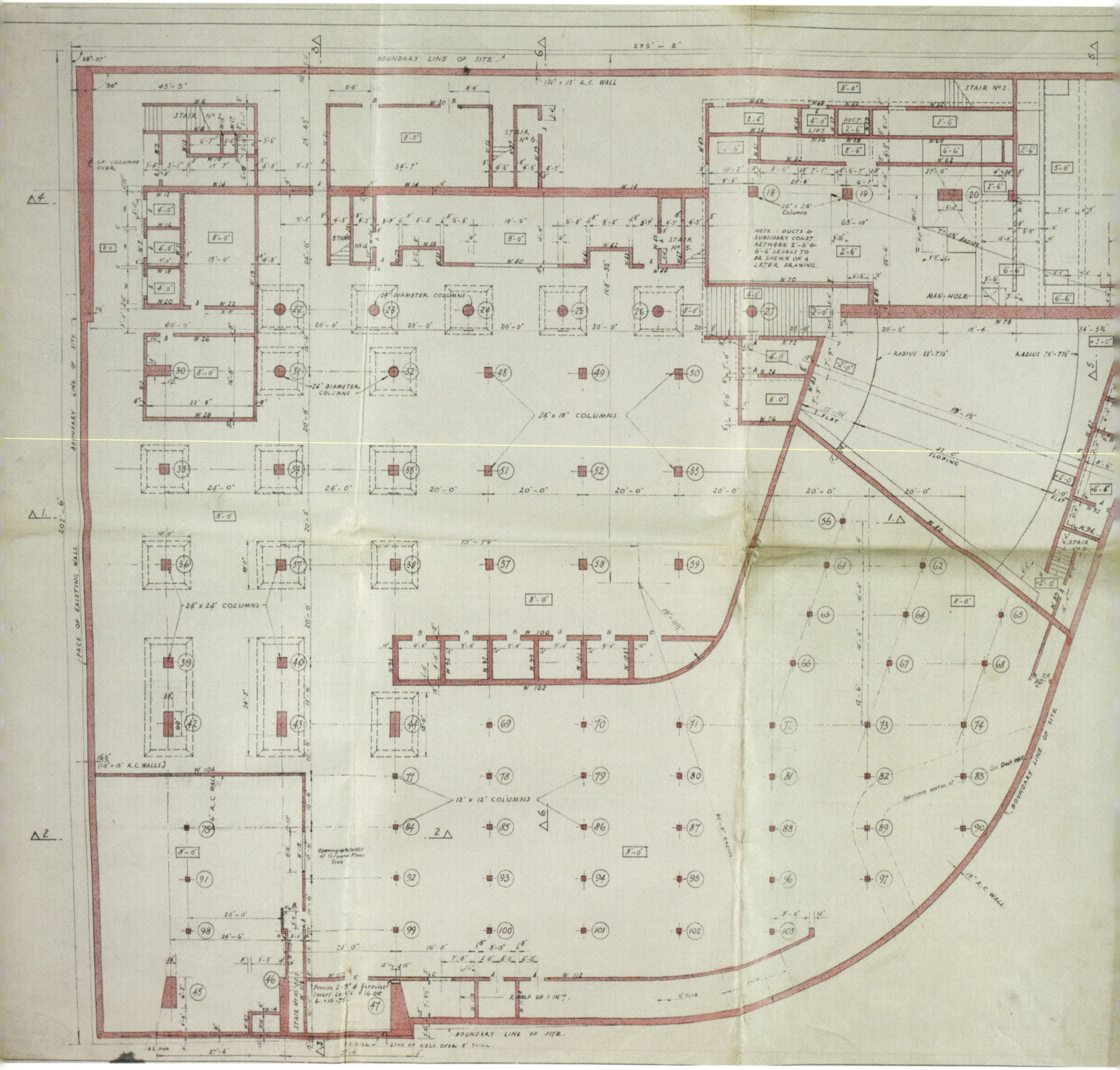

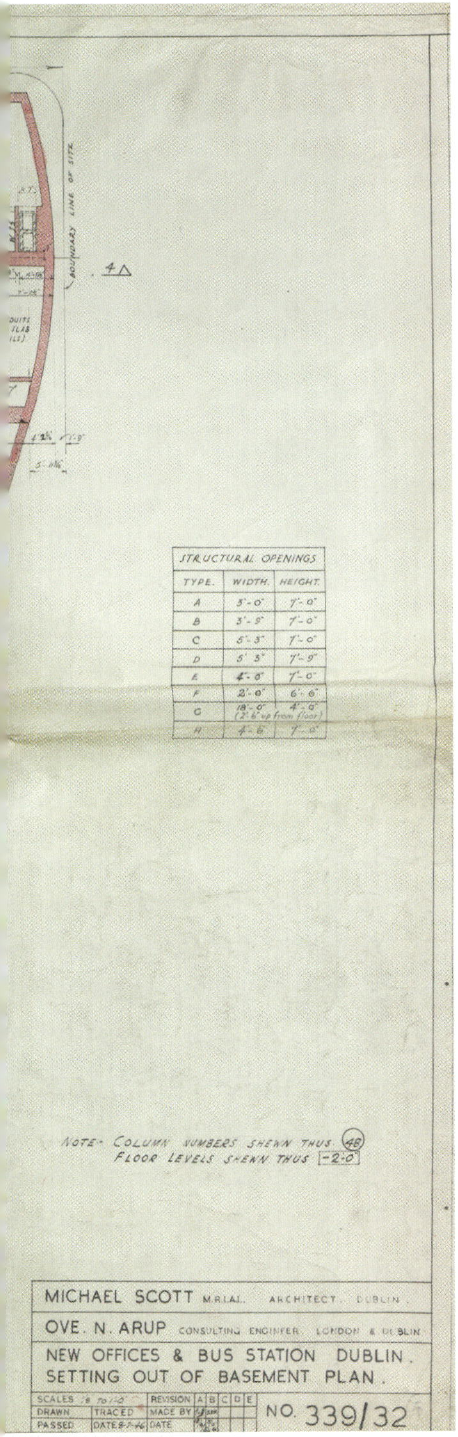

Battle over the Plans

With the site secured, CIÉ proceeded to appoint Michael Scott as the commissioning architect in 1944. According to Ciarán O'Connor, discussions between the bus company and CIÉ 'Produced a plan for a two-storey circular bus station on the site ... This was to have a concourse on the ground floor with a restaurant, booking offices, newsreel cinema and other facilities on the first floor.'[21]

Despite outline planning permission being granted, site clearance works commencing and CIÉ 'promising the travelling public that the station would be open within twelve months', by 1946 no detailed plans had been submitted to the corporation's planning committee.[22]

Finally, a revised design was submitted and put on public view in September 1946. The proposal was now to provide both a bus station and expanded office accommodation for CIÉ. The building was to have eight storeys, rather than two.

The Irish Times' planning correspondent, Ernest Aston, took exception to the proposal. A key member of the Greater Dublin Reconstruction Movement, Aston was no supporter of modern architecture. This was particularly the case in such close proximity to what was considered the jewel in the crown of the city's eighteenth-century built heritage, James Gandon's Custom House.

On 3 October 1946, *The Irish Times* published a photo montage of the Custom House with the new bus station office block looming large in the background. The height and impact of the bus station as pictured in the montage were significantly out of proportion to the new building's actual scale. Scott initiated legal action against the newspaper and, in 1947, secured an apology, legal costs and the original glass plate of the image, which was broken into pieces to ensure the image was never printed again.

Unfortunately, *The Irish Times* was not the only critic of the proposed building. Dublin Corporation's planning committee had concerns and rejected the plan by a single vote. Scott and CIÉ appealed the decision to the corporation's General Purposes Committee. Following consultation with the Royal Hibernian Academy and the Royal Institute of Architects of Ireland, the larger committee approved an amended design in 1947.

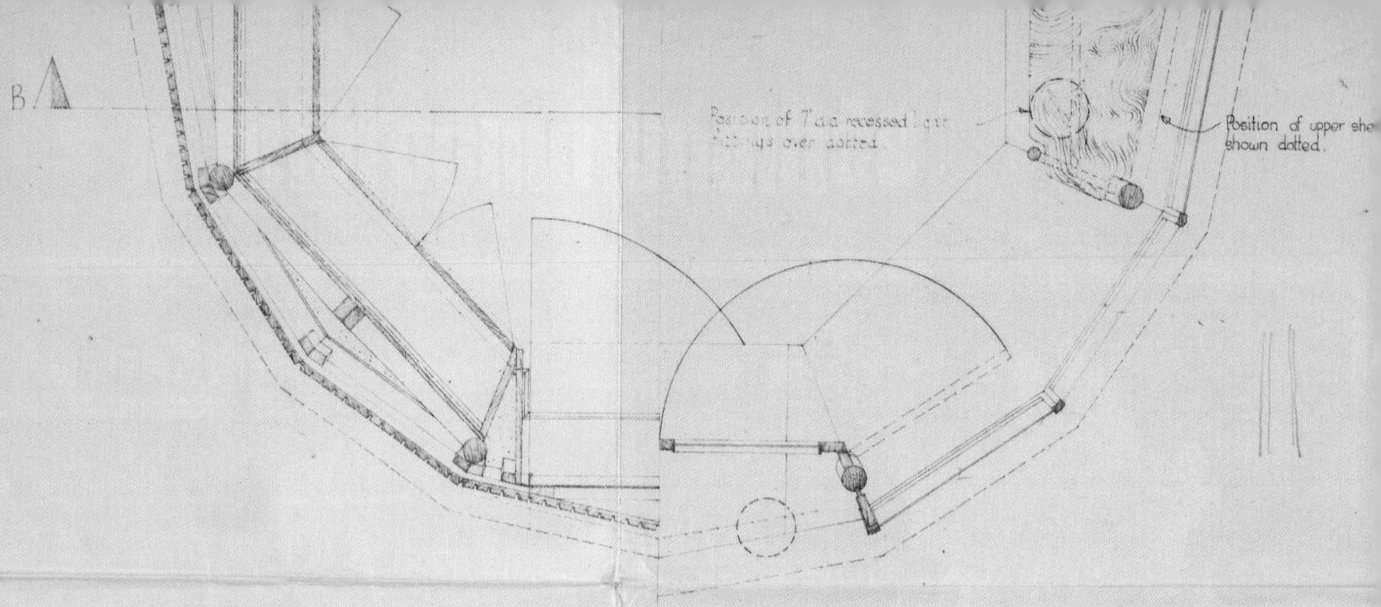

HORIZONTAL SECTION A-A.

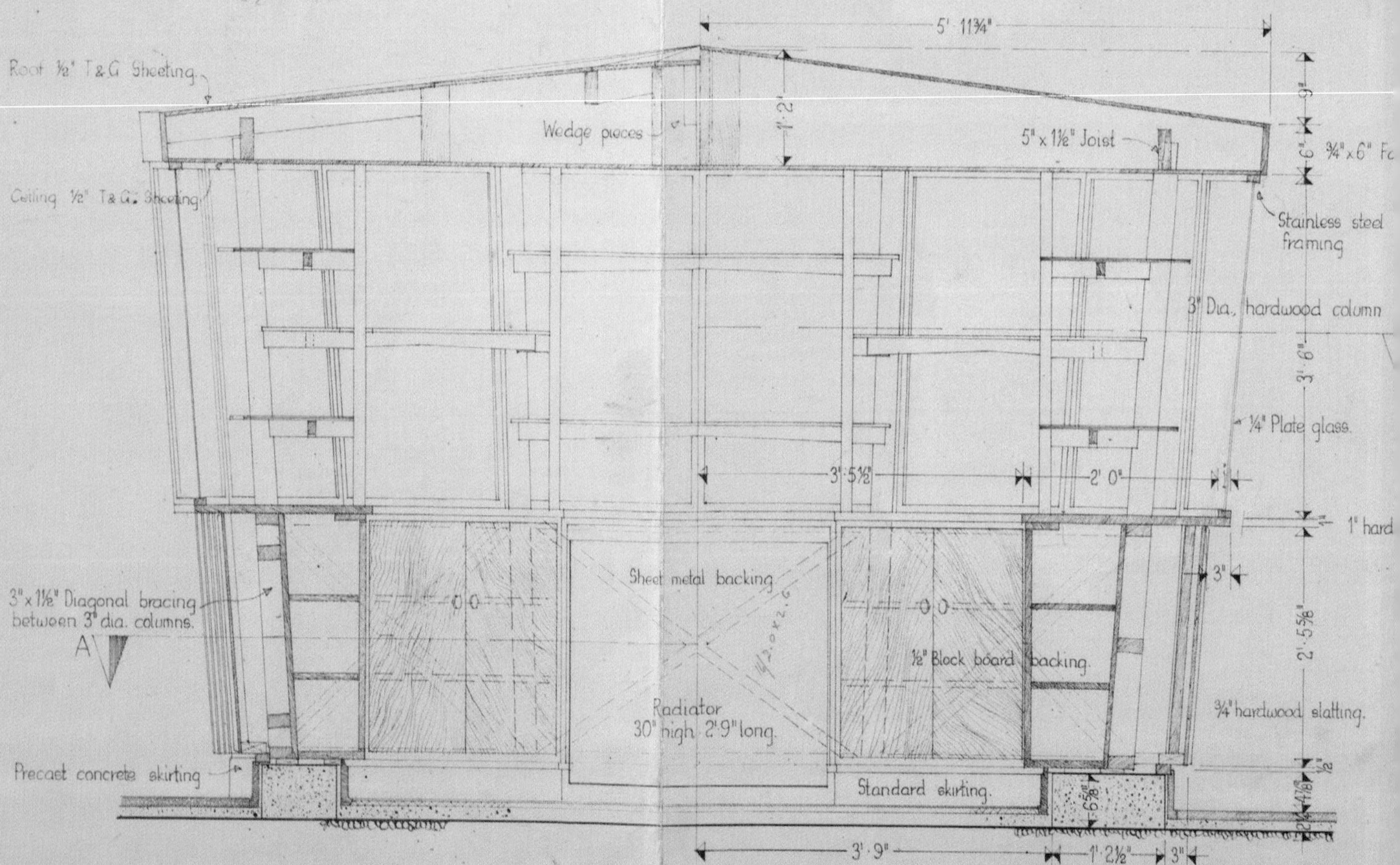

CROSS SECTION B-B.

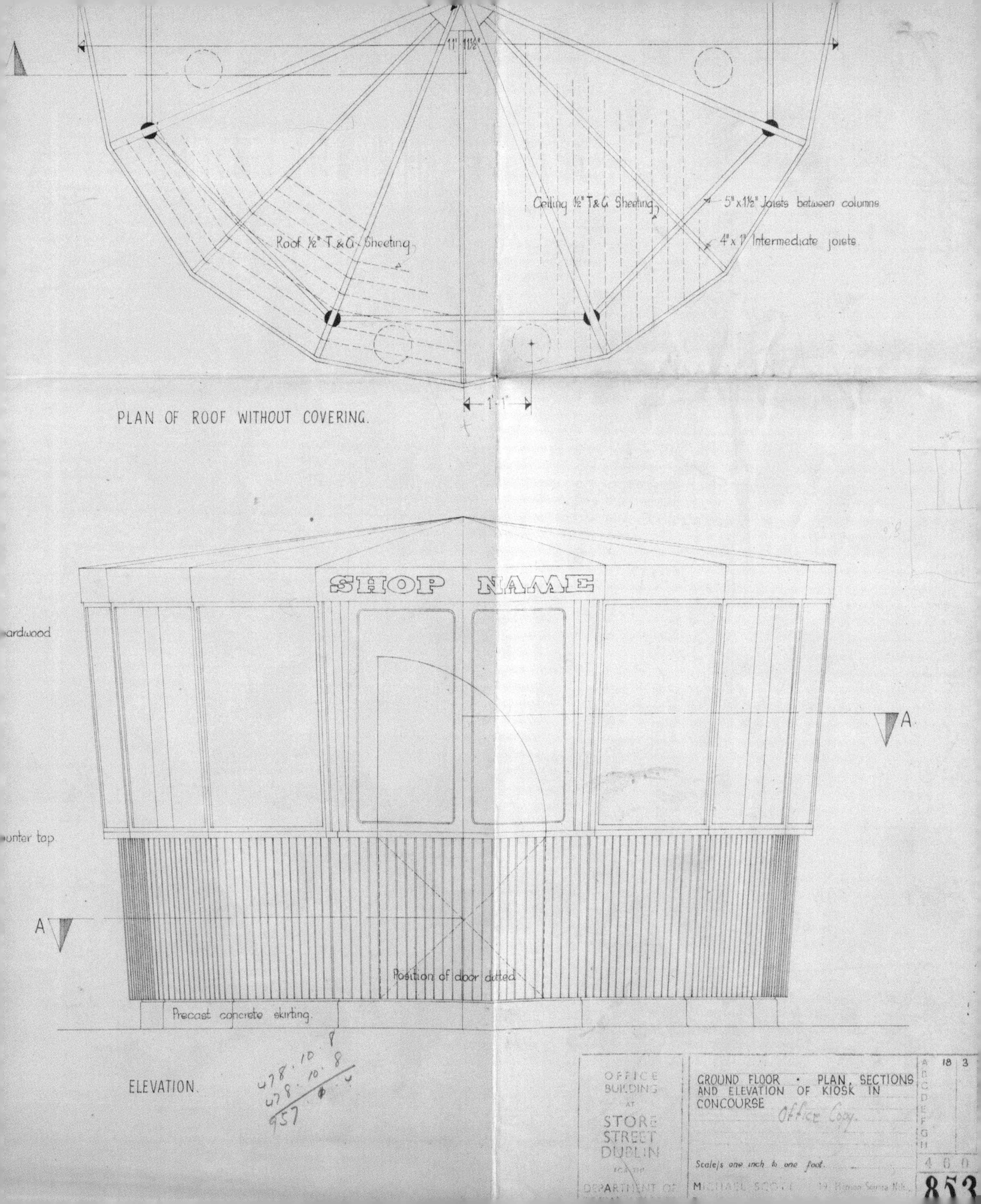

11'-11½"
Ceiling ½" T&G Sheeting
5" x 1½" Joists between columns
4" x 1" Intermediate joists
Roof ½" T&G Sheeting
1'-1"
PLAN OF ROOF WITHOUT COVERING.
SHOP NAME
ardwood
unter top
A
A
Position of door dotted
Precast concrete skirting.
ELEVATION.
478 . 10 . 8
478 . 10 . 8
957
OFFICE BUILDING AT STORE STREET DUBLIN
DEPARTMENT OF
GROUND FLOOR · PLAN, SECTIONS AND ELEVATION OF KIOSK IN CONCOURSE
Office Copy.
Scale/s one inch to one foot.
MICHAEL SCOTT
18 3
4 6 0
853

The height of the office block at the rear of the building was to be reduced as, according to Clerkin, 'the length of the city's fire ladders and rights to light on Store Street dictated that the main block's height be lowered'.[23]

No sooner had construction commenced than further controversy struck. CIÉ's accounts for 1947 showed a million-pound loss. O'Connor comments, 'As a result it became common opinion that the building was to be a white elephant and folly for such a cash strapped company. So when the general election of 4 February 1948 brought in a new coalition government ... it was decided not to proceed with the project in its original form and work was halted.'[24]

The political battle that ensued between the new Fine Gael-led government and the Fianna Fáil sponsors of the Central Bus Station was to last three years, during which time construction on the Store Street site halted completely.

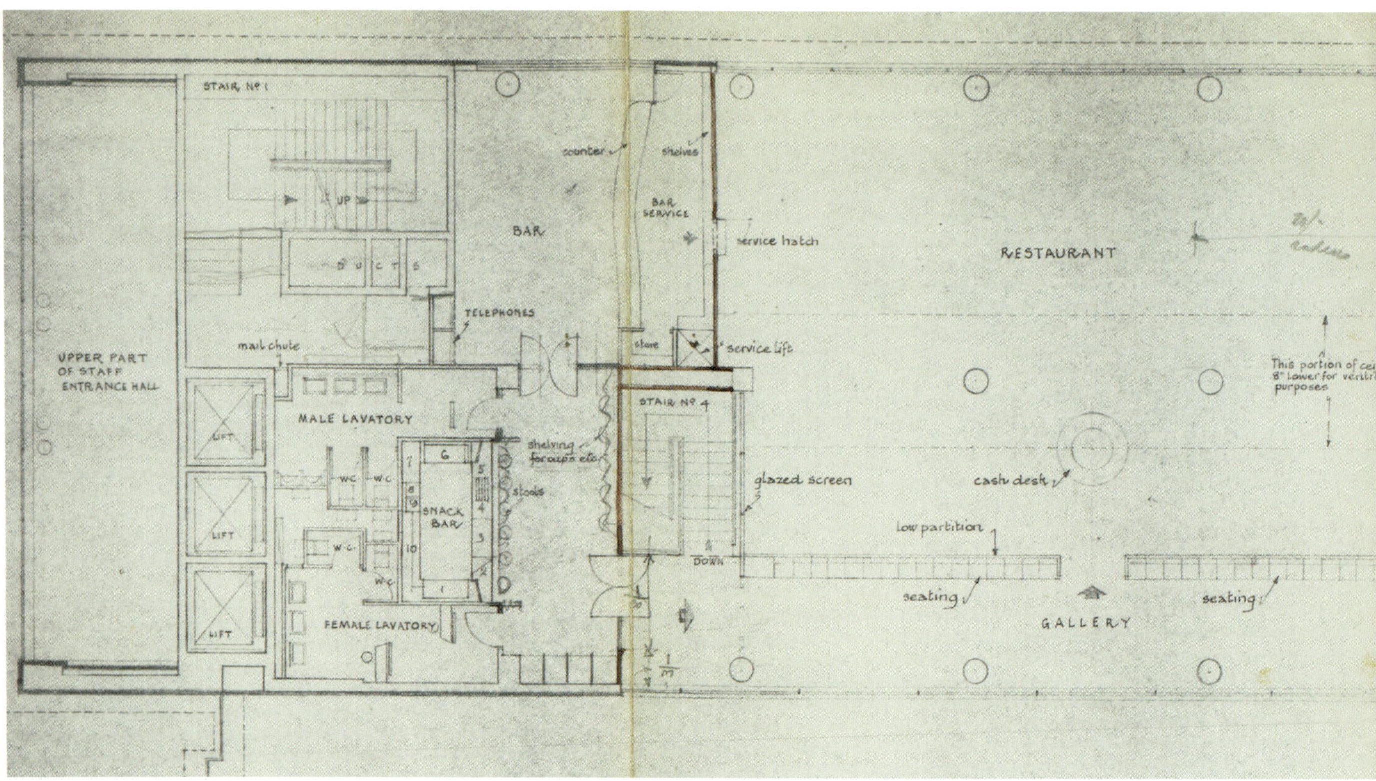

A Monument to the Previous Fianna Fáil Government?

Taoiseach John Costello appointed the former manager of the Great Western Railway, Sir James Milne, to review the bus station project. His recommendation was to abandon the Store Street site completely and develop a less ambitious project, 'making use of existing buildings in place of the proposed new chassis maintenance and body building shops at Broadstone'.[25]

Of course, construction was too far advanced at that stage for the government to completely walk away from the project, so instead it decided to use it for government offices. Clerkin quotes the then Fine Gael minister for finance, Patrick McGilligan, who said that while 'Government had been unable to stop the project, they "hoped to turn it into some useful purpose"'. Clerkin argues, 'It was felt at the time that the building was very much a monument to the previous Fianna Fáil Government and was resented as such by the current administration.'[26]

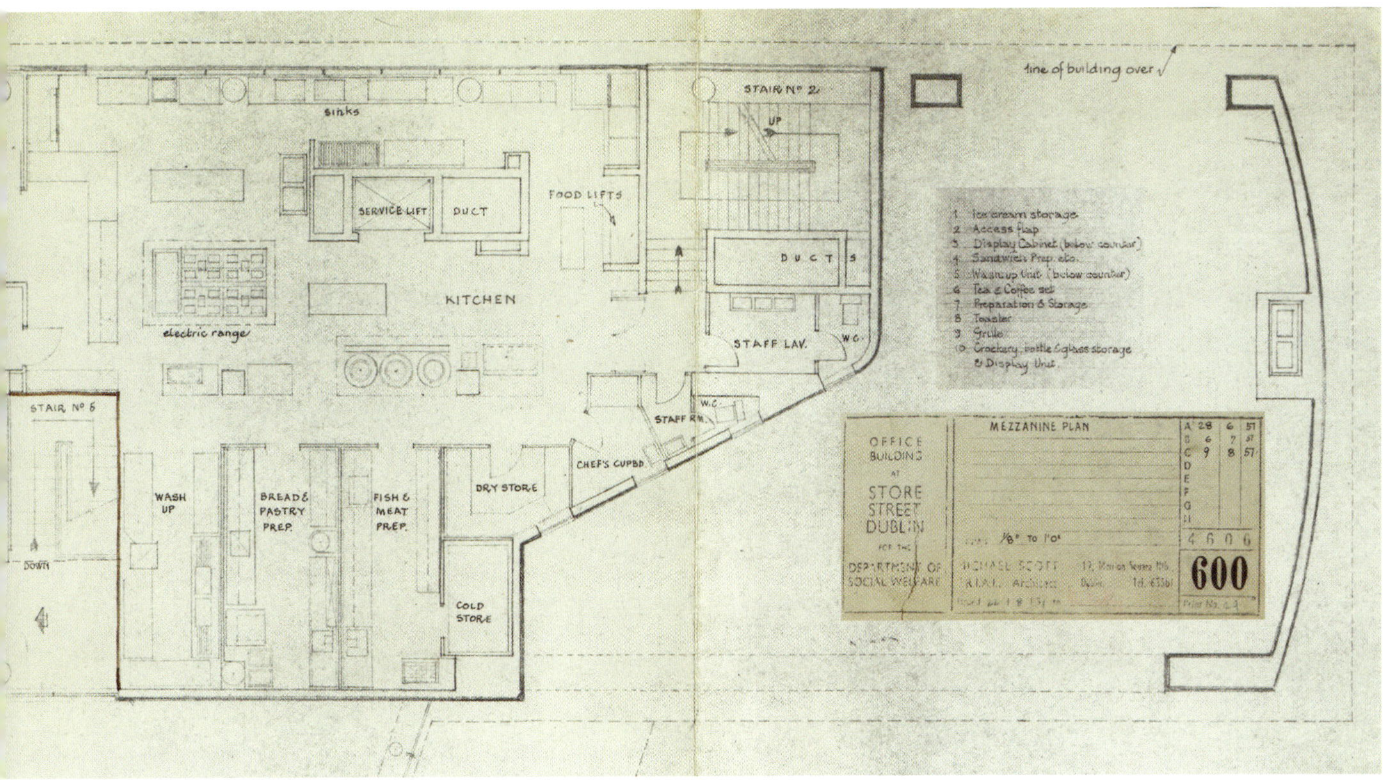

An *Irish Times* editorial opined that 'having been instigated by Fianna Fáil, there is a reluctance on the part of the Government' to see the project through.[27]

What ensued was a second round of wrangling as to where the new bus station was to be located. The government, supported by the planning correspondent in *The Irish Times*, wanted the new station to be located in Smithfield, where a more 'utilitarian' service would be provided. This was hotly resisted by members of Dublin Corporation, who, during a special council meeting, described the Smithfield proposal as 'daft' and driven by government interference.[28]

In December 1949, Alderman Hughes tabled a motion aimed at forcing CIÉ to return to the Store Street site and 'to have the project there completed and put into service as a Bus Station at the earliest possible date'.[29]

The heated exchanges on the floor of Dublin Corporation were also played out in Dáil Éireann. From the opposition benches, Seán Lemass railed against the government during a debate on the Transport Money Bill, describing 'the suggestion of establishing the Station at Smithfield as mad'.[30]

The angry political exchanges inside the Oireachtas were echoed by various interested parties protesting outside. Traders from Smithfield and Talbot Street both made the case for locating the new bus station close to their premises, as the resulting increased footfall would be good for business.

Not to be outdone by the politicians and the protestors, the letters page of *The Irish Times* was to provide a platform for a running commentary on the dispute. Michael Scott orchestrated a campaign of high-profile letters from the wider cultural community, including Louis le Brocquy and architect Uinseann MacEoin. Le Brocquy engaged in a lengthy argument with John Manning in which he extolled the virtues of the original concept and design:

> Dubliners are not merely to be denied all the thoughtfully planned amenities of this centre. They must also witness the mutilation of a building worthy to stand in dignity

> beside our Georgian Custom House – a unique building planned and made by our own citizens in the context of our time which can, as Collinstown already has, earn us the admiration of the world.[31]

Le Brocquy was correct in stating that the building, even in its unfinished form, was attracting attention from international architects. Having visited the site in Store Street, the editor of the Royal Australian Institute of Architects journal, Robin Boyd, wrote a glowing feature on the building, describing it as a 'distinguished contribution to the development of imaginative modern architecture'.[32]

Meanwhile CIÉ was having its own problems. Beset by growing financial losses, the transport company was fully nationalised. Faced with falling revenue, it no longer needed the large-scale office space that was to be provided in the Store Street development.

There was much speculation as to what the future function of the half-built office block would be. According to Clerkin, newspapers suggested the building, when completed, could house An Garda Síochána or the Department of Posts and Telegraphs, or even Raidió Éireann, the state broadcaster. Eventually the Taoiseach announced that the building would be home to the future Department of Social Welfare, one of the new innovations of a coalition government that included the Labour Party and Clann na Poblachta. There was even talk of using the bus concourse as a women's labour exchange.

As 1950 was coming to a close, the *Irish Times* editorial expressed the general public frustration at the ongoing dispute, declaring that 'The people's patience is not everlasting.'[33] Thankfully, political events intervened again. The coalition government collapsed and Fianna Fáil returned to power in the general election of June 1951.

Having campaigned to complete the bus station in Store Street, the newly elected Taoiseach, Éamon de Valera, announced 'the restoration of many beneficial projects stopped or curtailed by the previous Government, including the use of the Store Street buildings as a Central Bus Station'.[34]

2
BOT

A Much-changed Project

While Fianna Fáil ensured the Store Street development would recommence, it was a much-changed project from the one that had ground to a halt in 1948. With CIÉ's ambitions curtailed by new financial realities, and the decision to co-locate the new Department of Social Welfare with the bus station now agreed upon, the original vision of French and Scott was fundamentally altered.

Clerkin rightly reminds us that during the 1950s bus travel was much like air travel is today: people arrived early and waited for considerable periods of time before their departure. Aware of this, Scott and Reynolds wanted to ensure that the travelling public had the very best of amenities while they waited. According to Clerkin, 'CIÉ set out to make the building a microcosm of the city, a mini city within the city, with all the facilities that the passenger could possibly want in the mezzanine and basement, including an arcade of shops and a cinema.'[35]

Unlike the Collinstown Airport, which catered for the wealthy few, bus travel was transport for the masses, and Scott and Reynolds believed that working people travelling to and from the provinces should have access to the very same amenities and services in the Central Bus Station as did the wealthy visitors travelling in and out of the airport. Originally, there was to be a crèche, barber's and small chapel, a range of shops and two restaurants including the rooftop balcony with spectacular views of the city. All of these amenities were located in a building deliberately designed to provide the maximum comfort and leisure for the waiting public.

Under the revised plan, however, many of these facilities were scaled back or completely removed. While the political battle with Fine Gael and their supporters in *The Irish Times* was now over, Scott would have one final round of tussles, this time with the secretary general of the Department of Social Welfare, Dan O'Donovan, over details of design, materials and cost.

Throughout the final years of the building's construction, a furious exchange of correspondence from both Scott and O'Donovan made their way to the office of the minister for social protection, James Ryan. The matters under dispute were wide-ranging, and included the final division

of the building, the amenities to be provided to the public, the material to be used in certain locations, the design of the furniture and, of course, the all-important question of cost.

In September 1952, Scott wrote to Minister Ryan expressing concern that O'Donovan was forcing 'radical change in the use of portions of the building', resulting in 'depriving the public of one of the amenities in the Bus station, namely, the Barber's shop'. Scott was concerned that the secretary general 'does not understand that the development of an idea from its inception to its realisation in a final drawing takes considerable time' and, because of this lack of understanding, 'the building is again to be threatened, and the Bus Terminus and its amenities to the public to suffer ...'[36]

O'Donovan was equally trenchant in his criticism of the architect. Writing to the minister in October 1952, the secretary general lamented Scott's 'bitter and personal opposition which he has expressed in his letter to you'.[37]

O'Donovan went on to defend the decision to prevent bus passengers having access to the rooftop restaurant on the basis of needing to have a 'clear-cut division of the premises' between CIÉ and the department. O'Donovan was also highly critical of Scott's choice of 'certain marble and very expensive wood finishes for the floors of the staff restaurant', which he described as 'extravagant' and which would result in 'unanswerable criticism' being directed towards the minister in due course.[38]

Further correspondence was issued in November 1952 from O'Donovan, followed by letters from Scott in December, and then a detailed memo from the secretary general to the minister in February 1953. Scott and O'Donovan quarrelled over every detail of the building, its use and its fittings, leading to the latter making a formal complaint to the Institute of Architects that year.

The final dispute centred around the signage for the building in advance of its formal opening. Scott had commissioned leading typographer Colm Ó Lochlainn to design the lettering for the building's name plate: Áras Mhic Dhiarmada. In the end, a dispute between Scott and O'Donovan on the proposed location of the lettering resulted in Ó Lochlainn withdrawing from the commission.

Although O'Donovan won each of the disputes, arguing that he was simply carrying out government decisions, Scott was determined to have the last word. Writing to the Taoiseach to complain about O'Donovan's 'anachronisms in design and planning', the architect made it clear that he would point out to any visiting architects that he was not responsible for such flaws.

The Bus Station Finally Opens

A final delay in the completion of the project was caused by an unofficial electricians' strike in support of industrial action being taken by the workers in CIÉ's bus and train maintenance department.

Finally, on 19 October 1953, seven years after construction started and more than fifteen years after the site was first proposed, Dublin's Central Bus Station finally opened. The total cost was in the region of £1,000,000, a staggering bill for any building at that time.

Described by the *Irish Independent* as 'Dublin's Wonder Building', the opening of Áras Mhic Dhiarmada and Busáras generated significant domestic and international news coverage. According to O'Connor, 'all the daily newspapers devoted upwards of six pages', with articles focusing on the 'cost, statistics about glass and square feet of floor area and photographs of the interiors'.[39]

Architects' Journal described the placement of this modernist building in a primarily Georgian setting as a 'bold architectural gesture', comparing it to a similar project by leading Brazilian modernist architect Oscar Niemeyer.

A feature article in the *Irish Builder and Engineer*, whose attitude towards the building during its construction was agnostic, to say the least, was much more complimentary now that it was completed. The nine-page special opened with a glowing endorsement:

> This fine building, uniquely combining the functions of Government offices and a central bus station, was formally opened by the Tánaiste Mr S. Lemass, who rightly said that the occasion was one of some significance in our history and that the new building would take its place among the many fine buildings for which Dublin was famous; already it has secured international recognition for its architectural achievement and Mr Scott and all those who had contributed to its construction could be proud of it.[40]

For Michael Scott, the completion of the project was an occasion for mixed emotions. Reflecting some years later, he told friend and art critic

Dorothy Walker: 'That building took so much out of me.' He continued, 'I designed it to be the most modern building that could be produced with the most modern technology.'[41] Elsewhere, Scott concluded that it 'must be reckoned the principal work of my architectural career'.[42]

Dublin finally had its Central Bus Station, and Scott and his talented team had completed their finest architectural achievement to date. But the final building was not what Reynolds or Scott had set out to accomplish. The many changes that occurred during seven long years of controversy – in design, function and cost – were to fundamentally change the relationship between the travelling public and their bus station, denying them access to some of its most important architectural and design features while narrowing the experience from that of a 'microcosm of the city' to something more utilitarian in nature.

But at least passengers no longer had to queue in the rain on Custom House Quay waiting for their bus to the provinces.

Today

Sixty-eight years later and Áras Mhic Dhiarmada and Busáras still functions as the headquarters of the Department of Social Protection and Bus Éireann's provincial bus route station. The buses are bigger and, pre-COVID, passenger numbers higher, but the drivers still enter the west gate, exit the north gate and park along the original passenger gates.

The seating in the concourse has been replaced and the kiosks removed, but the design is essentially the same. The mezzanine restaurant was converted into a ticket office and now lies empty. Automated machines dispense tickets instead of a busy-staffed ticket office, and a small number of shops remain. Much of the office space in the station remains unused, in contrast to the busy offices in the neighbouring department.

The underground newsreel closed in 1959, after which the space was occupied by the Eblana Theatre; it staged shows right into the 1990s. Much of its programme was filled with works by young Irish playwrights, such as the stage adaptation of J.P. Dunleavy's *The Ginger Man*, as well as dramas by Friel, Keane and Beckett.

THIRTYTW
Uisce Domhain
Deep Water

According to artist and curator Gavin Murphy, who has researched the history of the theatre, while the Eblana wasn't 'very cutting edge', it was home to 'plays that were critical of the Irish Catholic Church, of society's views on unmarried mothers, on contraception, homosexuality', all taboo subjects at the time.[43]

In 1962, the Eblana staged Tennessee Williams' *The Rose Tattoo*. Phyllis Ryan's Gemini Productions show was the first outing of the play since it was banned by the censor in 1957 on its opening night at the Pike Theatre. The last play to be performed at the Eblana was *Return to the Hill*, the sequel to Lee Dunne's gritty novel adaptation of *Goodbye to the Hill*, about life in working-class Dublin. If you venture into the theatre today, underneath the layers of dust there are still programmes and casting notes, untouched since the play's last night.

Like much of the building, the underground theatre is still in good structural shape. Indeed, one of the striking features of the building as a whole is that, despite the lack of investment over the years, it has stood the test of time. All of its main functions remain intact and operational.

Despite this, its most impressive features remain off-limits to the public. The sixth-floor rooftop restaurant with its beautiful mosaic murals and stunning views of Dublin is for civil-service staff only. The mezzanine restaurant is long closed, now filled with dusty boxes and stacks of broken furniture, its viewing gallery into the bus station concourse blocked by a large, grey blind. The underground theatre remains locked, layered in dust, with an, as yet, uncertain future.

It is not hard to understand why so much of the beauty of this building remains unseen when the travelling public is literally not allowed to see it.

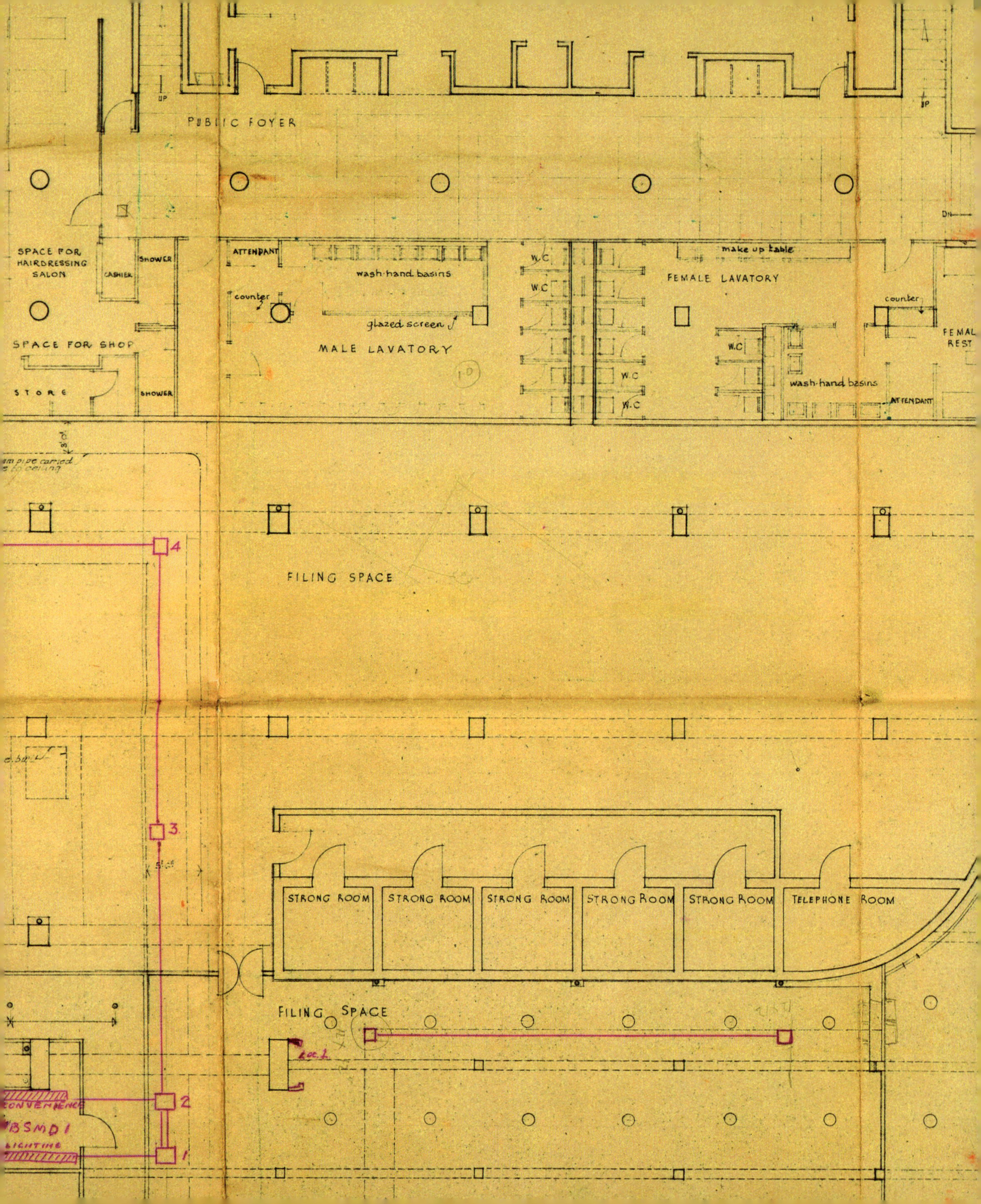

PUBLIC FOYER
UP
SPACE FOR HAIRDRESSING SALON
CASHIER
SHOWER
SPACE FOR SHOP
STORE
SHOWER
ATTENDANT
wash-hand basins
counter
glazed screen
MALE LAVATORY
W.C
W.C
make up table
FEMALE LAVATORY
W.C
W.C
W.C
wash-hand basins
ATTENDANT
counter
FEMAL REST
DN
FILING SPACE
4
3.
STRONG ROOM
STRONG ROOM
STRONG ROOM
STRONG ROOM
STRONG ROOM
TELEPHONE ROOM
FILING SPACE
2
1
CONVENIENCE
BSMD I
LIGHTING

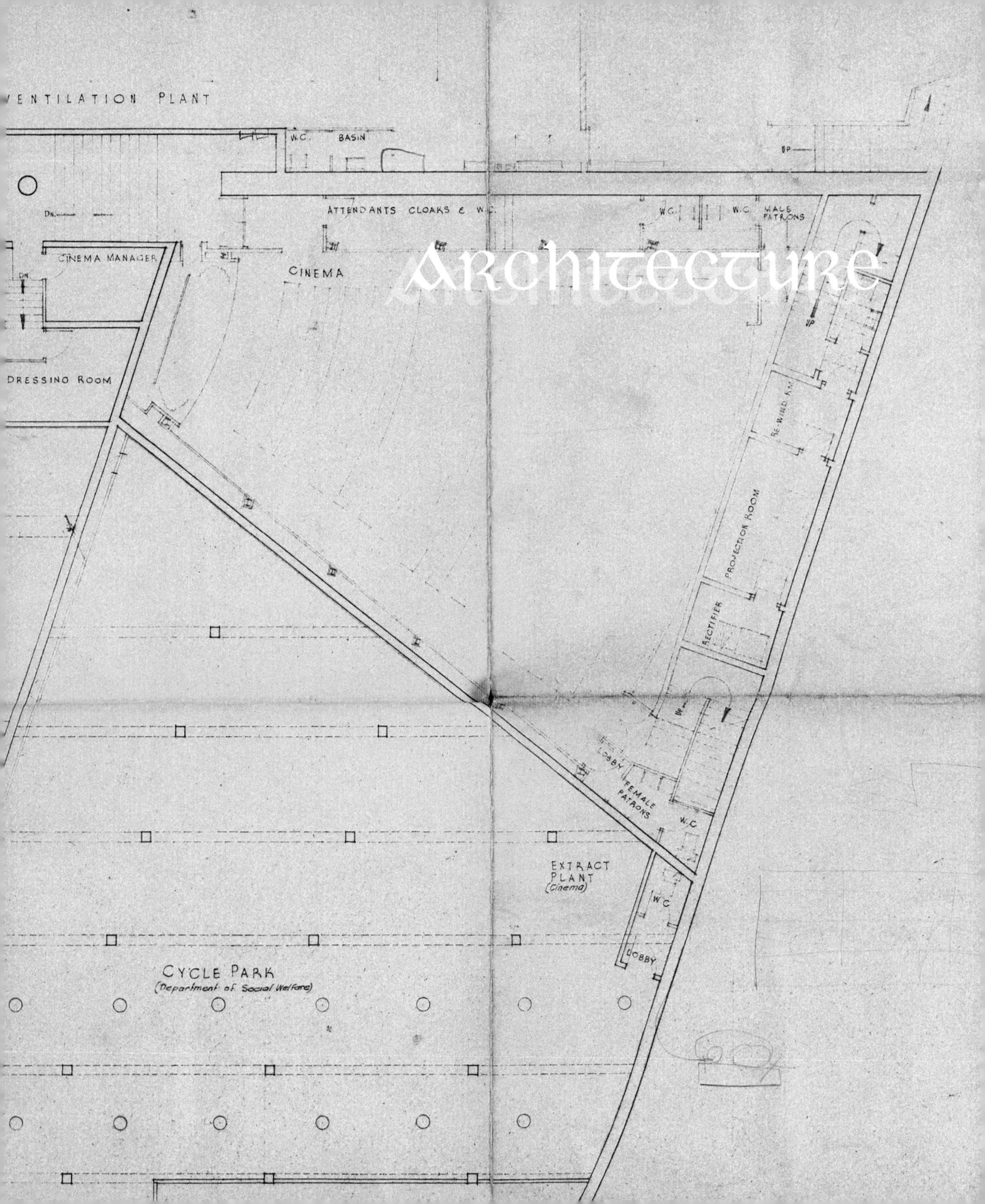
VENTILATION PLANT
W.C.
BASIN
UP
ATTENDANTS CLOAKS & W.C.
W.C.
W.C. MALE PATRONS
CINEMA MANAGER
DN.
CINEMA
DRESSING ROOM
RE-WIND RM
PROJECTION ROOM
RECTIFIER
UP
LOBBY
FEMALE PATRONS
W.C
EXTRACT PLANT
(Cinema)
W.C
LOBBY
CYCLE PARK
(Department of Social Welfare)

SCANIA

Architecture

You employ stone, wood and concrete, and with these materials you build houses and palaces; that is construction. Ingenuity is at work. But suddenly you touch my heart, you do me good, I am happy and I say, 'This is beautiful.' That is Architecture. Art enters in.

Le Corbusier

The Dublin architectural scene in the 1930s and 1940s was a mixture of neoclassical tradition and an emerging embrace of modernist trends from continental Europe and Scandinavia. The quality of training was high and there was an awareness of international developments arising from annual educational trips to the Netherlands, Germany and France organised by the School of Architecture at University College Dublin. Students and professional architects had access to the latest developments through architectural journals and books, as well as visiting lectures organised by the Architectural Association.

In conversation with Dorothy Walker, Michael Scott recounts his own initial exposure to some of these developments: 'Somewhere at the end of the twenties or early thirties, Frank Yerbury [the acclaimed architectural photographer] came to the Architectural Association of Ireland and gave a lecture on Swedish architecture. That was the first time that I became conscious that there was, or could be, an interesting form of modern architecture.'[1]

Some years later, Scott, now president of the Architectural Association, hosted the German architect Walter Gropius, founder of the

Bauhaus art school, in Dublin. The trip took place in 1936, during which time Gropius gave a talk on his latest book, *The New Architecture and the Bauhaus*. Scott was later to describe the enormous impact the visit had on his own development: 'The Bauhaus was a remarkable event in the history of architecture. It had a dramatic impact on the whole creative world. When I became aware of it, I really began to understand what I was doing.'[2]

Gropius' short and concise book outlined the key principles of what he described as the 'new architecture'. Changes in building and engineering technology were liberating architects and giving them a greater 'mastery of space'.[3] In particular, steel frame, concrete and glass were revolutionising the making of buildings. Architects were less reliant on the use of internal walls to support structures, giving them ever greater access to space and light.

The result was 'a progressively bolder (i.e., wider) opening up of the wall surfaces, which allows room to be much better lit', replacing 'the old type of window' with 'continuous horizontal casement, subdivided by thin steel mullions'. For the architect, this meant more 'voids' and less 'solids', providing what Gropius termed a 'sparkling insubstantiality'.[4]

Along with more space and light, the new materials offered another advantage: greater standardisation. In the years between the two great wars, the cost of providing much-needed housing and other key public infrastructure projects became a growing concern.

Gropius told his readers, 'The elementary impulse of all national economies proceeds from the desire to meet the needs of the community at less cost and effort of its productive organisations.' Increased mechanisation in construction would, in the architect's view, 'abolish the individual's physical toil … in order that hand and brain be set free for some higher order of activity'.[5]

At the same time, the use of new modular technologies for construction should result in 'a happy architectonic combination of maximum standardisation and maximum variety'.[6]

Central to the Bauhaus vision was the combination of the most modern advances in industry, materials and technology with high quality

Expressway
www.buseireann.ie

craftsmanship and design, to provide products on a mass scale. The school's teaching programme sought to combine 'imaginative design and technical proficiency'.[7]

Heavily influenced by pioneers of the English Arts and Crafts movement, such as William Morris and John Ruskin, Gropius wanted to reconnect art with everyday life, banishing the 'heresy that art is just a useless luxury' and 'reuniting the world of art with the world of work'.[8]

Architecture, for Gropius, was not just about the construction of buildings, but should involve a 'union of all the different arts'. 'Our ultimate goal,' he concluded, 'was the composite but inseparable work of art, the great building, in which the old dividing line between monumental and decorative elements would have disappeared for ever.'[9]

The New Architecture and the Bauhaus stressed the importance of collective team effort in any architectural project. Great architecture was not the result of one creative mind or the 'pooling knowledge and talents'. Rather, the Bauhaus 'ideal was that what each collaborator contributed to the common task should be something he had devised as well as wrought himself'.[10]

Gropius extolled the Bauhaus virtue of 'the common citizenship of all forms of creative work, and their logical interdependence on one another in the modern world'.[11]

Importantly, Bauhaus was not intended to be a 'style, system, dogma, formulae or vogue' but rather 'a revitalising influence on design'. Indeed, for Gropius a 'Bauhaus Style would have been a confession of failure' and a return to 'stagnation and devitalising inertia'.[12]

In the final page of his book, Gropius writes of the relationship between tradition and the 'New Architecture'. He argues firmly that modern architecture is 'in no sense in opposition to Tradition', but respecting those traditions 'does not mean the complacent toleration of elements' or 'domination by bygone aesthetic forms'. Rather, such respect involves 'the preservation of essentials in the process of striving to get at what lies at the back of all materials and every technique, by giving semblance to the one with the intelligent aid of the other'.[13]

In her biography of Gropius, Fiona MacCarthy talks of the influence of Viennese architect Peter Behrens on the evolution of the Bauhaus

RÚNAÍ

Architecture

founder's ideas. Behrens developed the concept of *Gesamtkunstwerk* – the total work of art – in which every aspect of a building, including the design of its interior, furniture and decoration, is integral to the whole.[14] MacCarthy also emphasises the importance of William Morris' 'championing of art for the people' as being 'close to the democracy of creativity that [Gropius] himself espoused'.[15]

All of these key ideas can be seen at work in Michael Scott's Áras Mhic Dhiarmada and Busáras. Scott set out to design the most modern building that the latest materials and technology would allow. The building was designed around light and space, not mass and walls. Every aspect of the building, from the structural frame to the interior details, was integral to the whole. Art, in the form of mosaics and the use of colour, was essential to the building. And, crucially, the process was collective, with each creative partner contributing to what was intended to be a total work of art.

It is hard to fully appreciate just how radical Gropius' ideas would have been to young architects in the 1930s. So many of his principles, like those of other modernist masters including Le Corbusier, are now standard principles of architecture. But to the classically trained young professional, in a city of neoclassical and Georgian architecture, the Bauhaus principles were earth-shattering.

Speaking of the New Architecture, Walter Gropius was right when he said that 'Youth has been fired with its inspiration.'[16] Ireland in the 1930s and 1940s was no exception.

Free-state Modernism

While Scott and his collaborators may only have become familiar with the principles of architectural modernism through the late 1930s and early 1940s, the origins of the modernist movement in Irish building can be tracked back to the earliest years of the Free State.

Paul Larmour's *Free State Architecture* traces the evolution of Irish modernism from 1922 through to 1949. From the 'proto-modern' granaries built in Waterford, Westport and Dublin City at the turn of the century to the impressive hydroelectric plant at Ardnacrusha built

during the 1920s, innovation in design and technology was already evident.

Some of the most impressive examples of modernist architecture detailed by Larmour include Barry Byrne's Church of Christ the King in Turners Cross, Cork, built between 1927 and 1931, and a series of buildings for the newly established state Electricity Supply Board designed by Vincent Kelly in the early 1930s.[17]

While many of the early modernist buildings were factories or public buildings, a small but distinct number of residential homes were also constructed during this period. Joseph Downes' flat-roofed houses on Kincora Road, Clontarf, and a series of elegant, one-off homes in Howth, Sutton and Glasnevin by a variety of architects borrowed heavily from the early years of the International Style.

Public housing was also influenced by new European developments, with Dublin Corporation chief architect Herbert Simms designing a series of modernist flat complexes in the inner city following a study trip to the Netherlands.

According to Larmour, the real advance of modernist buildings came during the 1930s and 1940s. Increased investment in local hospitals and colleges of technology brought European modernism, with a very strong Irish feel, to the provinces. Works inspired by this movement included the Nenagh General Hospital, Naas Fever Hospital and Limerick's Tuberculosis Institute, all by Vincent Kelly and built during the early 1930s.

Scott was himself involved in a number of these projects, including the granite-clad County Hospital in Tullamore. As detailed earlier, he was also involved in a number of private-sector projects, including a series of regional buildings for the Ritz Cinema chain.

Larmour argues that, following the 'pioneering days of the 1920s and 1930s', there was a growing diversity of new architectural practice showing 'not only the versatility of the Modern Movement but also the variety of expressions and form' demonstrating 'the vital relevance of modern architecture to modern life in Ireland'.[18] Larmour's conclusion is worth quoting in some detail:

> From its early beginnings to its eventual arrival as a dominant force, the Modern Movement in Irish architecture produced a comparatively small but significant body of work, including much of considerable quality and interest. This was an architecture which essentially sought to achieve forms of universal significance, and yet, in the context of a new state seeking

> to establish its way in the world, can be seen at times to take on an almost consciously national identity which had little to do with traditional forms or historic ornament, but all to do with national pride and independence of spirit.[19]

While Desmond Fitzgerald's design for the Collinstown Airport in Dublin exuded this sense of 'national pride and independence of spirit', it would be Scott's Central Bus Station that would be the most complete example of what modernism could bring, not just to Irish architecture, but to public service provision and Free State nation building.

The Busáras Team

In some respects, attributing Áras Mhic Dhiarmada and Busáras to Scott is a misnomer. A large group of very talented architects, designers and engineers worked on the project. A number of them were principally responsible for key aspects of the building we know today.

Scott, however, was not only able to spot and encourage exceptional talent, but his entrepreneurial skills and ability to network ensured that the ideas of his team were realised. His confidence and ability to convince others were indispensable to ensuring such an ambitious project would succeed. Similarly, his overall aesthetic vision for the project ensured a unity of form and purpose, despite the many individual approaches from within his chosen team.

Scott brought the same skill set to choosing and sourcing materials and expertise from Ireland and abroad as necessary.

While a number of architects worked on the design of the building, the key figure was Wilfred Cantwell. Clerkin argues that he 'was responsible for the way the building looks today'.[20] Having graduated from the University College of Dublin School of Architecture in 1944, Cantwell had two key attributes that made him ideal for the Central Bus Station project. His thesis was a design for new offices for the headquarters of the GSR in Heuston Station.[21] Indeed, it was through his father, who worked for the GSR, that Cantwell got his introduction to Scott.

More important was his attachment to the modernist aesthetic of the Swiss architect Le Corbusier. Cantwell remembers that 'The only books on modern architecture available at the college were a couple of books of Le Corbusier's. We always thought they were marvellous.'[22]

After initially working for Scott on McCairn's garage in Dublin City centre, Cantwell was brought onto the Busáras job. Two other members of the team, Barry Quinlan and James Nolan, had been struggling with an initial design which formed the first planning application to Dublin Corporation. Cantwell scrapped their cylindrical model for a larger L-shaped proposal, with the buses entering and exiting from the west and north respectively through portals at each end of the building. This design breakthrough not only set the shape of the building to be but was also central to solving the most significant problem involved with the site: namely how to ensure the successful flow of the buses into and out of the station given its tight location, marooned between three separate streets.

Beyond the technical merits of Cantwell's design, his building is typically Le Corbusier. Clerkin said that the architect 'worked with a book of Le Corbusier's work beside him' while at Busáras. Cantwell told Paul Clerkin that he 'based the design of Busáras on the Maisson Suisse', a student accommodation block for Swiss students in the International City University in Paris that he had seen during a trip to Paris in 1947.

Having completed the principal design, Cantwell left the project to start his own practice. The remainder of the work, including the detailed drawings of the office blocks and bus concourse, was done by Kevin Fox and Paddy Hamilton.

On the engineering side, Scott took the view that this was an area requiring international expertise. After considering a number of options, the decision was taken to invite Ove Arup to Dublin to work on all three of the CIÉ projects. The London-based architectural engineer would prove a decisive appointment as he brought a number of key innovations to the bus station, including the now-iconic curved concrete canopy that covers the station concourse and embarquement area.

Cantwell described the Arup canopy as 'a unique feature, not like anything done before'. It was important for the canopy to extend far

enough out from the internal concourse to keep the passengers dry as they boarded the buses. However, according to Cantwell, 'a flat canopy would have required a massive counterbalancing weight, so it was not feasible'.[23] The innovative solution was to have incredibly thin-set concrete carrying its own weight through carefully calculated curves.

This was not just the first time such a technique was used, but it made possible further advances by Arup on world-famous buildings, such as the Sydney Opera House.

Arup was also important in recommending that Scott employ the services of the Varming company, which in turn employed the Irish engineer Sean Mulcahy as the services engineer. Both Arup and Varming subsequently established offices in Dublin that continue to operate today.

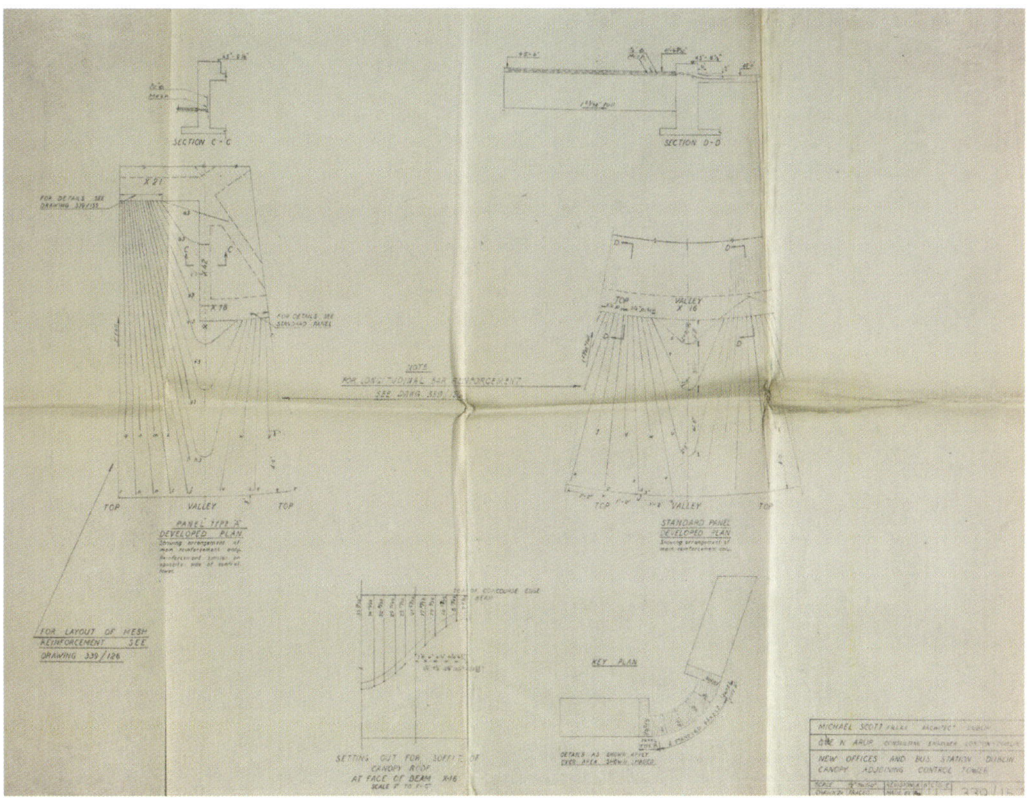

Architecture

An Architectural Tour

In November 1953, the *Irish Builder and Engineer* ran a detailed special on the new Áras Mhic Dhiarmada and Busáras. The sixteen-page feature included nine pages of text and photographs, and seven pages of advertisements for the various suppliers and companies who worked on the station.

The article acknowledged that both the nature of the site and the corporation's height restrictions 'conditioned the general design', while the 'C.I.E. accommodation requirements governed the architect's solution'.[24] The article goes on to comment that, on a site of less than an acre, the architect had to design accommodation for at least 800 office workers, a marshalling yard for up to seventeen buses and a large public assembly space complete with a variety of amenities for the public. The architect's solution to this large demand on such a small site was:

> An L-shaped plan ... with a north block of 140 feet x 55 feet, the public hall being provided by roofing in part of the space between the two arms of the L and the marshalling yard occupying the remainder of the space with the busses entering under the southern end of the western block and leaving through the eastern end of the northern block.[25]

Architectural historian Ellen Rowley attributes part of the final design of the building to the geometry of a bus turning, just as Le Corbusier had determined much of the shape of his iconic 1935 Villa Savoye from the geometry of the single turn of a car.[26] Sufficient space was left for double-decker buses to enter the yard through a fifty-foot gateway below the west block. The supporting structure for the entrance was made from dark Swedish granite and Irish Kingscourt brick. Buses would reverse-park into the passenger gates before moving off to exit the building from a similarly designed gate on the north side of the building.

Irish Builder and Engineer highlighted the 'striking shell concrete canopy that is such a distinctive feature of the building ... which is finished in blue, has a 20-foot overhang that affords adequate shelter for passengers disembarking from the buses'.[27] The canopy is just two and a

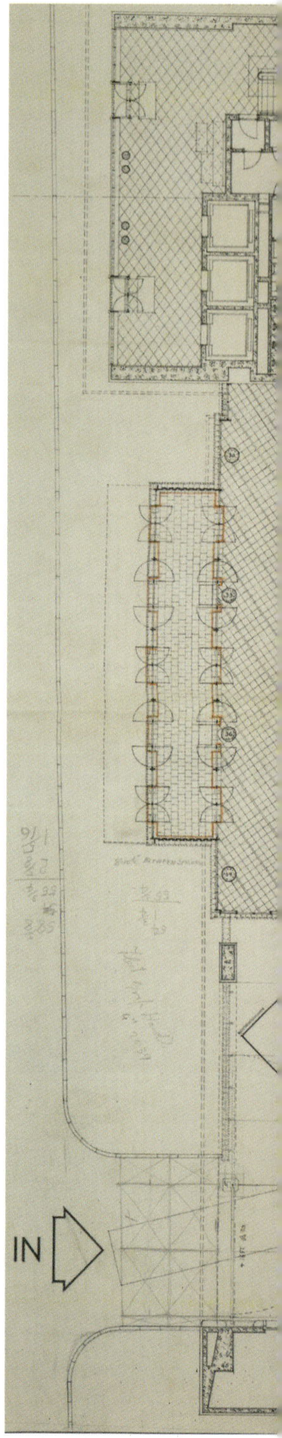

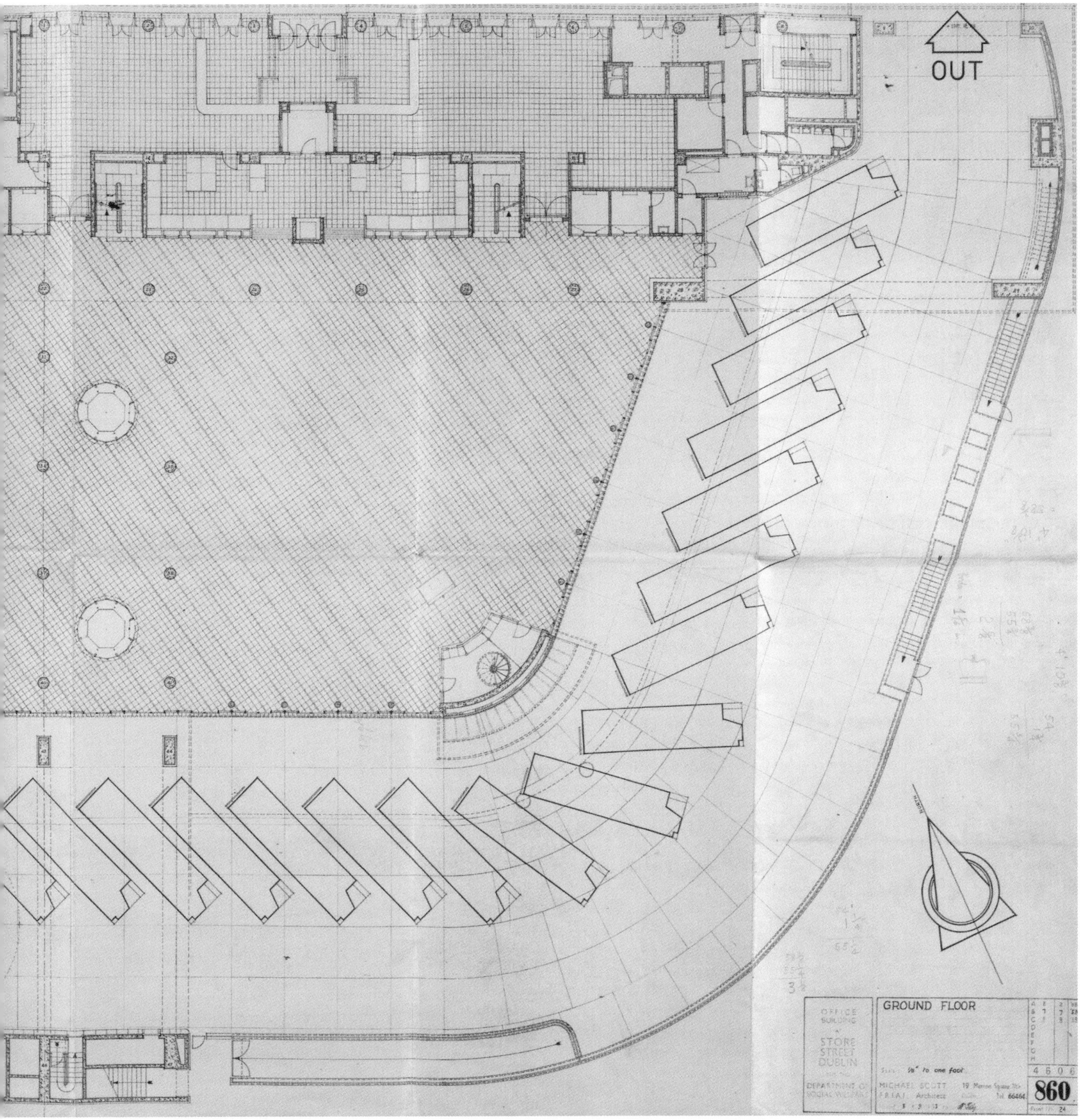
OUT
GROUND FLOOR
OFFICE BUILDING
STORE STREET DUBLIN
1/8" to one foot
4606
860

Architecture

half inches thick, and the curves have a depth of thirty inches and a pitch of ten inches.

The site's proximity to the River Liffey required a very specific form of foundation to avoid flooding. This was achieved with the use of a reinforced concrete raft foundation below sea level. The outer faces of the foundations are further waterproofed by an asphalt lining. The basement sits eleven feet below street level and is made of eighteen-inch reinforced concrete, strengthened to thirty-six inches under the building's columns.

Above the foundation, and taking in the ground floor of the bus station, the building was to rise to seven storeys in the north block and four storeys in the west block. The principal office block on the north comprised two seven-storey façades of Portland stone. Scott's original intention was to use granite. However, cost and unreliability of supply from local quarries led the architect to opt for the less expensive

Portland stone from England. The move, though motivated by cost, was incredibly fortuitous.

The Custom House, adjacent to Áras Mhic Dhiarmada and Busáras, was also built from Portland stone. The use of the same material in a building which was antithetical to its eighteenth-century neighbour in almost every other aspect of its design softened the otherwise jarring nature of its proximity. Indeed, the use of Portland stone was read as an explicit reference to Gandon's Custom House, leading the *Irish Builder and Engineer* to conclude that 'these so widely dissimilar buildings should form reasonably good neighbours in spite of their opposing styles'.[28]

The Portland stone on both gables rested on the ground-floor layer of narrow red Kingscourt bricks, which were also used extensively in the building's ground floor, adding warmth to the façades and surrounding street-level views.

At the front gable on Store Street, the footpath-level corners were adorned with black stone mouldings, the purpose of which was unclear but which added a nice additional aesthetic detail.

Plate-glass glazing set in bronze frames was used on both sizes of the two office blocks. The 700 windows were estimated to have 60,000 square feet of glass. This led the *Irish Builder and Engineer* to speculate that it made 'the Store Street building amongst the largest users of plate glass in the British isles'.[29]

Work on the foundations and concrete structure started in 1946. John Sisk and Son was the principal contractor. More than 300 tradespersons worked on the building in addition to an unknown number of subcontractors. Work on the outer shell was completed within a year, and the cost of the foundations and building was estimated at £200,000, about a fifth of the final cost of the entire scheme.[30]

The plate-glass glazing also separates the north block from the bus station passenger concourse with an internal glass-and-bronze-frame wall. The south-facing wall of the concourse is also a glass-and-bronze frame, creating a flood of light into the 10,500-square-foot area. This vast open space is supported by a series of large columns.

Passengers, while waiting for their bus, could avail of a 140-seat restaurant on the mezzanine floor, from which they could look down onto the concourse. Alternatively, they could descend the stairs to the baggage area from where they could also access the 200-seat, twenty-four-hour newsreel cinema. The bus station also included a bar, snack bar and number of kiosks.

The offices in the main block were open plan and 240 feet long by 50 feet wide, though demountable partitions allowed for subdivision. The exception was the third floor, which held the offices of the minister for social protection and related staff. The entire building was air-conditioned and had modern inbuilt sprinkler systems in case of fire, as well as a centralised vacuum-cleaning system.

The *Irish Builder and Engineer* was particularly enthused by these innovations, describing how 'Air was taken from the top of the building through pierced faience blocks and drawn down shafts to the basement, 120 feet below, where it was drawn through oil filters and then scrubbed

by jets of water, after which it was warmed and circulated through the building.'[31]

The temperature was set at a standard eighteen degrees Celsius and automatically controlled by an external master thermometer. The temperature was further regulated by an unusual system of double glass-plated windows, separated by a two-foot gap containing heating coils, that assisted in heating up the building during colder months while preventing condensation between the double windows. The inner panes could be opened, while the permanently closed outer panes protected the offices from dust, a particular problem given the building's proximity to the docks and Connolly train station.

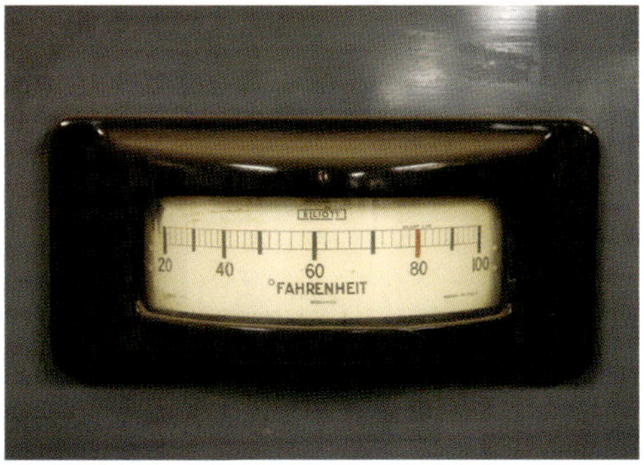
ELLIOTT
20 40 60 80 100
°FAHRENHEIT

ELLIOTT
0
0
SET TO 0 AFTER USE

60 80 100 40 32 120

From the outside of the building, this double-window system gives the building a distinctive look, particularly as light is reflected and refracted through both sets of plates. Clerkin suggests that 'there is a horizontal rhythm formed by the white bands of Thermoloux in the window frames [which] create an egg-crate effect'.[32]

The ministerial floor had a number of distinctive features, including a number of self-contained balconies. The sixth floor was home to the Department of Social Welfare's staff canteen, which also included a balcony.

Twelve contractors took out advertisements in the *Irish Builder and Engineer* special edition. Irish companies including Sisk, Roadstone, Boylan insulation and air-conditioning specialists and Mills scaffolding were prominent, as well companies from overseas, such as Hathernware, which supplied the faience. Dublin Verso Brothers, which supplied the terrazzo, and electrical contractors Doherty Ltd also featured.

Assessment

Larmour describes Áras Mhic Dhiarmada as the 'first major work of modern architecture' in Dublin that was 'Stylistically a comprehensive exercise in the modern style, and designed with distinction and elegance.'[33] It set 'new standards of construction and servicing in Ireland'.[34] For his efforts, and that of his team, Scott was awarded the Royal Institute of Architects of Ireland Triennial Gold Medal in 1958.

Merlo Kelly in *More than Concrete Blocks* says that Busáras 'is considered to be the zenith of Ireland's mid-century architecture' due to its 'building technology and lavish use of materials'. He also confirms that it was one of the only buildings to attract international critical attention, 'with building reviews appearing in architectural journals in America, France and Britain', as well as receiving study tours of architects.[35]

Kelly also makes the case that despite the use of styles, materials and professionals from outside of Ireland, the overall design 'represented an emerging Irish architecture'.[36]

Clerkin, in the most detailed study of the building to date, is more critical, arguing that 'although impressive' the long delay in the construction meant 'it was stylistically outmoded by the time of its completion'.[37] One of the consequences of this, according to Clerkin, was that Busáras 'got less attention than it deserved', as it 'looked back stylistically at Le Corbusier's work of the 1930s but using the technology and decoration of the 1950s'.[38]

For Ciarán O'Connor, the success of Busáras operates on two levels. On the first, the building works: for over sixty years it has functioned for the purpose it was designed, a bus station. Despite the tight site, and the heavy surrounding traffic flow, 'they got it to work ... operating on the flow of the traffic ... [and] with a clarity that is simple'.[39]

Beyond the function, for O'Connor the building expressed a bigger idea: 'it was an idealism of what we could do as a nation'. Like Collinstown Airport, Busáras was another 'funny-looking building' that 'looked forward'. It was 'modern while being respectful of the Custom House'.[40]

Michael Scott's son, Niall, followed in his father's footsteps, first into the architectural profession and then into his father's company,

SECTION – A·A.

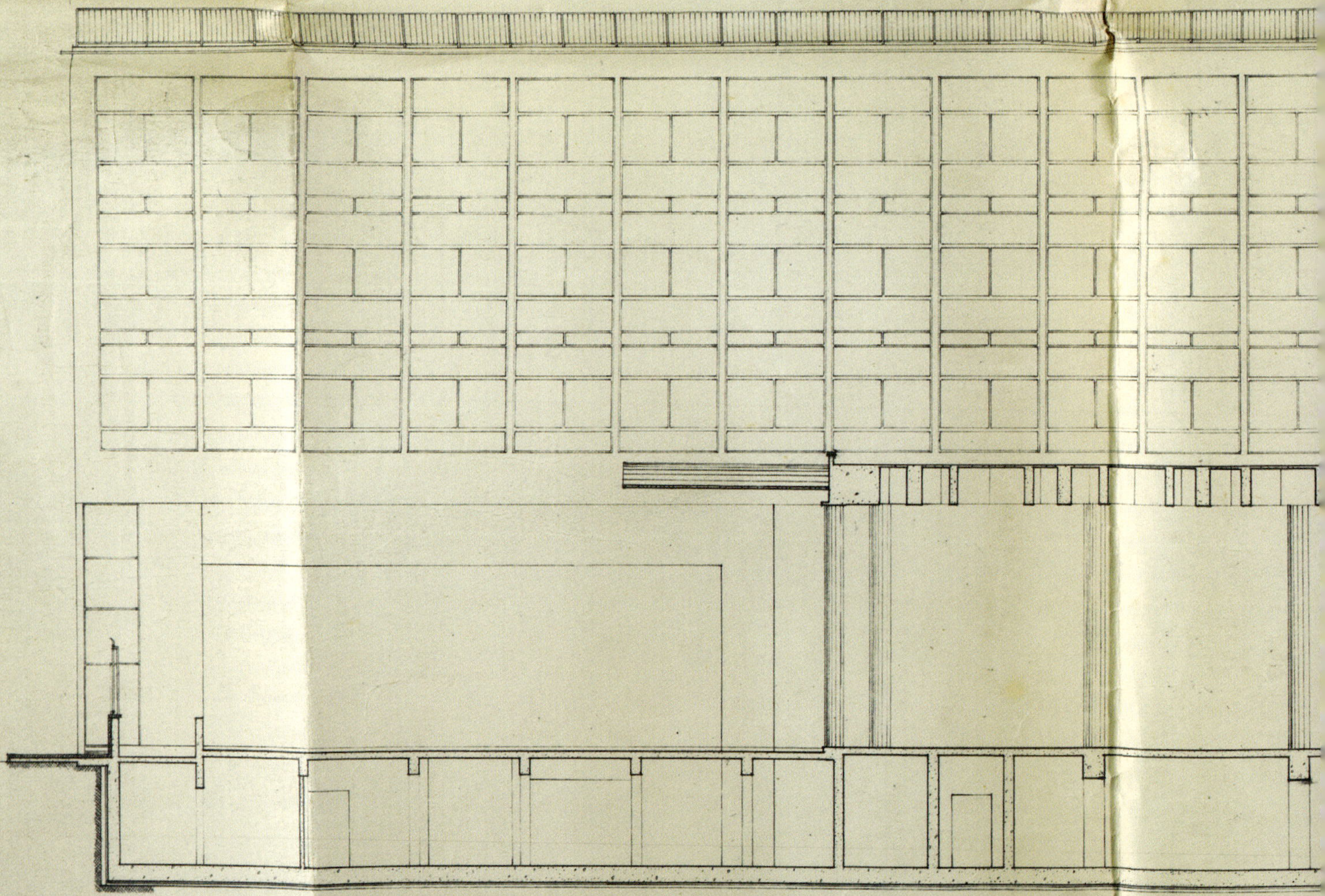

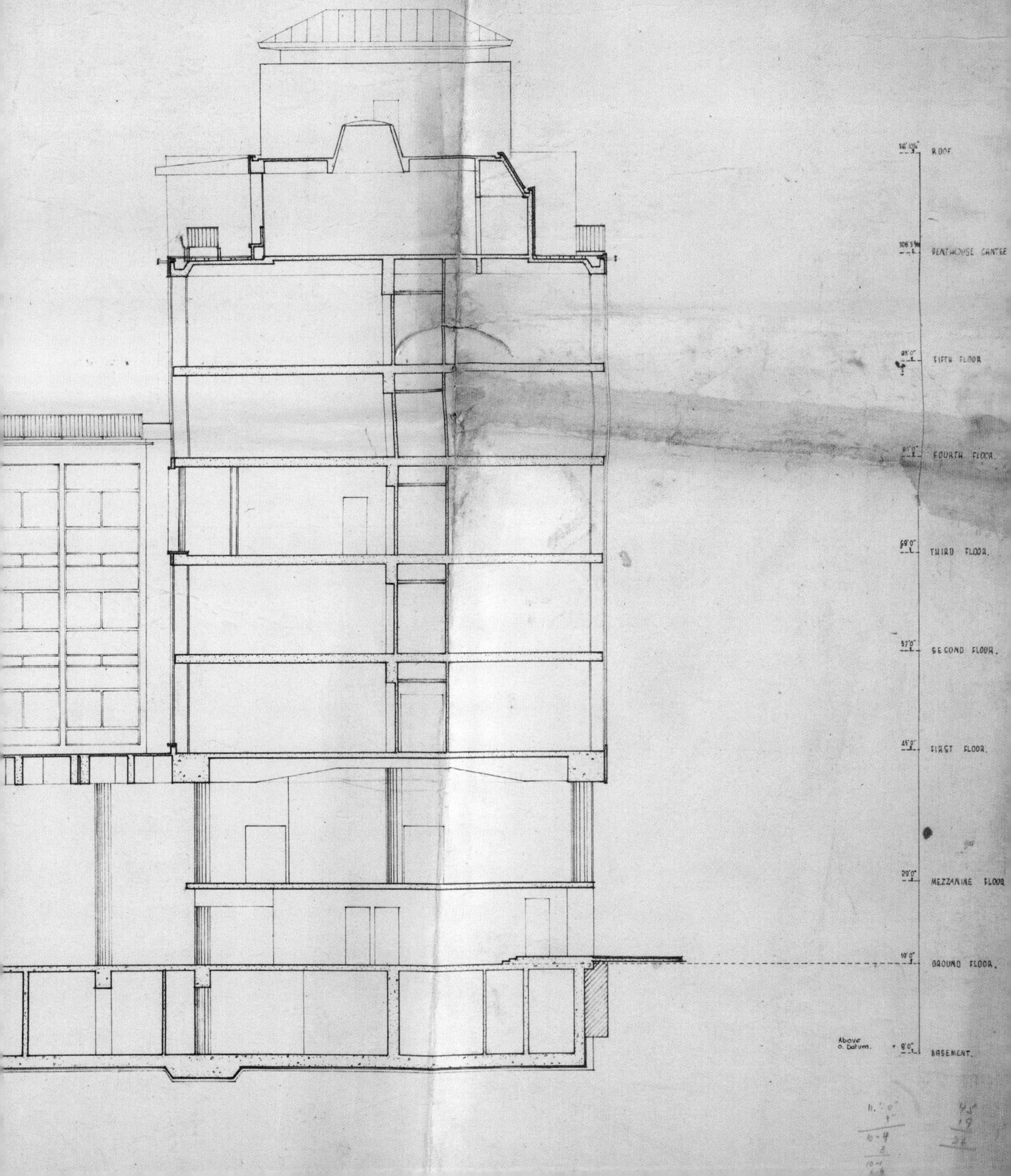
ROOF.
PENTHOUSE CANTEE
93'0"
FIFTH FLOOR
81'0"
FOURTH FLOOR.
69'0"
THIRD FLOOR.
57'0"
SECOND FLOOR.
45'0"
FIRST FLOOR.
29'0"
MEZZANINE FLOOR
19'0"
GROUND FLOOR.
Above
O. Datum.
+ 8'0"
BASEMENT.

Scott Tallon Walker. Now retired, Niall has vivid memories of being brought onto the construction site as a young boy in 1948. He shares O'Connor's view of the importance of the building's functionalism. 'The first thing in any building,' he told me, 'is that it should work, that's the fundamental thing; this building still works, it functions well.'[41]

As we chat about the building in the vacant mezzanine floor of the bus station, Niall still marvels at the building's attention to detail. 'Look at the elegance of the radiators,' he says. 'Everything you look at was beautifully put together, that's what architecture should be.'[42]

And, like O'Connor, he admires the way Busáras 'responded to the scale of the Custom House', respectful of it without being weighed down by it. 'Every age leaves down a layer' through its architecture, Scott tells me. 'That's what makes a living city, an exciting city.'[43]

For architectural historian Ellen Rowley, Áras Mhic Dhiarmada and Busáras was part of a short 'golden age' in modernist architecture in Ireland. For her, what is most impressive about the building is 'the location and the scale'. 'Can you imagine the size of this,' she said, 'how shocking it was?'[44]

This was the first modern building constructed in Dublin's city centre during the twentieth century. Earlier examples of modernist architecture, from the hospitals and technical colleges of the 1930s to the Collinstown Airport, were buildings 'on the periphery' outside the city. Rowley wondered if the island nature of the site 'enforced a negative effect ... alienating people from its surroundings', a feature that was to become ever more pronounced as the volume of cars, buses and eventually the Luas line intervened to disrupt the wider public's interaction with the building.[45]

There is no doubt that Áras Mhic Dhiarmada and Busáras was 'the principal work of [Scott's] architectural career'. In subsequent years he received a string of awards for his work, with the Central Bus Station at the forefront. Between 1967 and 1977, he received honorary degrees and membership from university faculties in the University of Ulster; the College of Technology in Bolton Street, Dublin; the Royal College of Art in London; Trinity College Dublin; the American Institute of Architects; and the Institute of Structural Engineers in London. In 1975, he was the

Bus Éireann

first Irish architect to receive the Royal Gold Medal for Architecture from the Royal Institute of British Architects. Similar awards were made in Iceland and Germany.

If Áras Mhic Dhiarmada and Busáras was the high point of Scott's architectural achievement, it was also to provide an important training ground and launch pad for some of the younger members of the team. Robin Walker went on to be one of the country's leading modernist architects in the subsequent decades, while Pat Scott moved from architecture to fine art, establishing himself as one of Ireland's most important twentieth-century painters.

Michael Scott consciously set out to create 'a great communal work of art'; it was intended to be 'a cathedral of the future', a modern, comfortable and beautiful amenity for the travelling public. That such an enterprise was even attempted in Ireland of the late 1940s is remarkable. That Scott and his team, despite all the obstacles, came so close, is worthy of celebration.

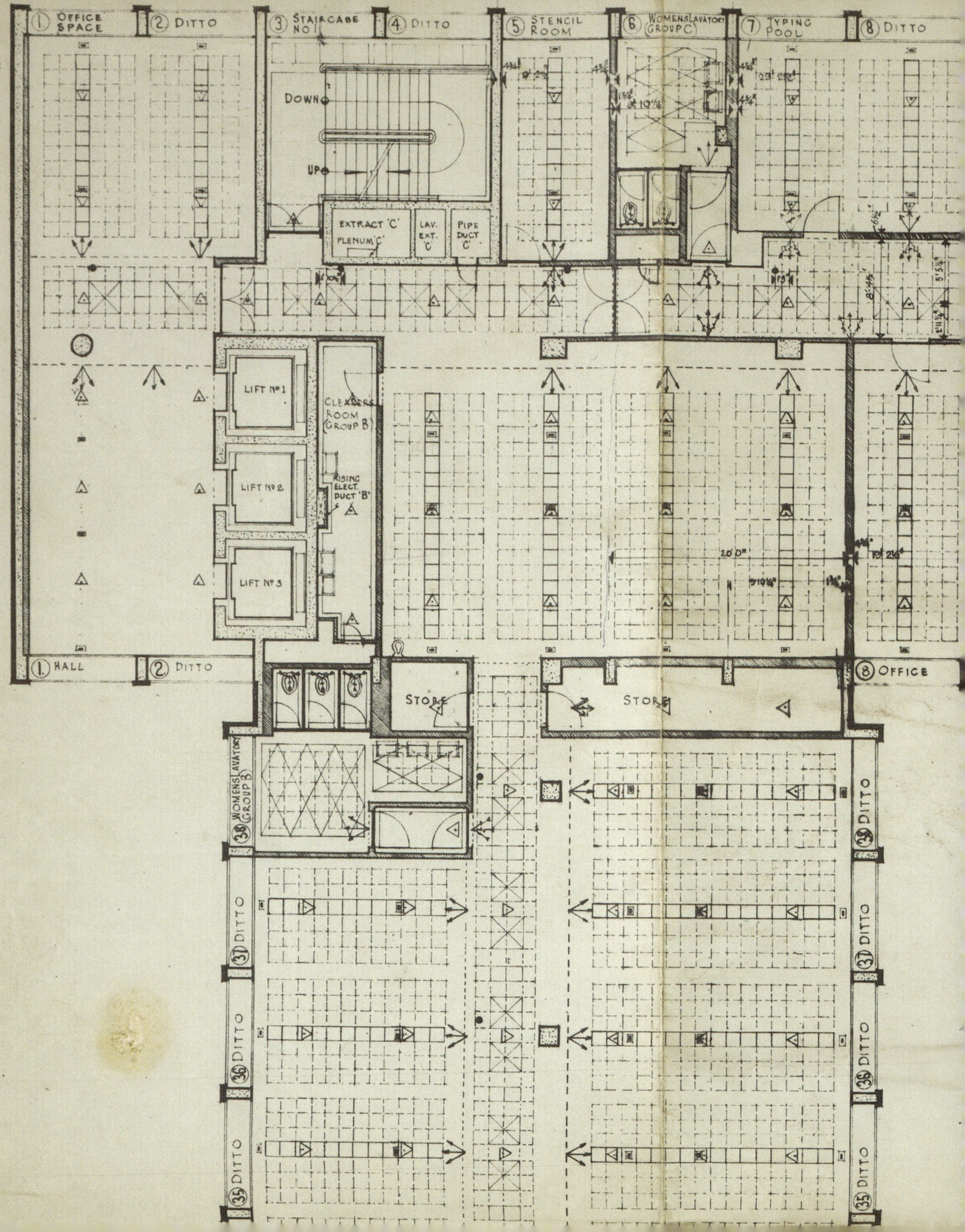

1 OFFICE SPACE
2 DITTO
3 STAIRCASE NO1
4 DITTO
5 STENCIL ROOM
6 WOMENS LAVATORY (GROUP C)
7 TYPING POOL
8 DITTO
DOWN
UP
EXTRACT 'C' PLENUM 'C'
LAV. EXT. 'C'
PIPE DUCT 'C'
LIFT No 1
LIFT No 2
LIFT No 3
CLEANERS ROOM (GROUP B)
RISING ELECT. DUCT 'B'
20'0"
1. HALL
2 DITTO
8 OFFICE
STORE
STORE
38 WOMENS LAVATORY (GROUP B)
38 DITTO
37 DITTO
37 DITTO
36 DITTO
36 DITTO
35 DITTO
35 DITTO

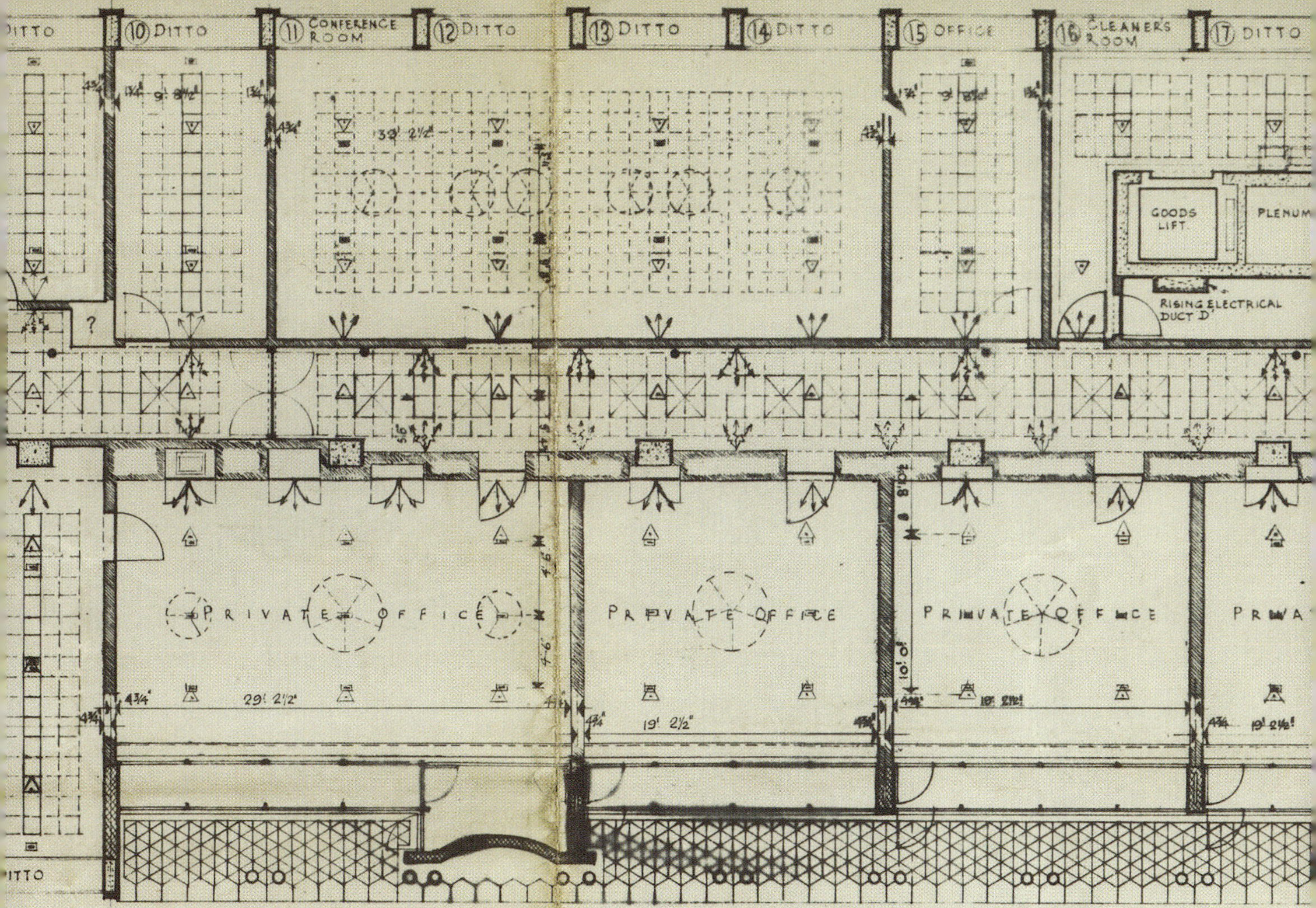

DITTO
10 DITTO
11 CONFERENCE ROOM
12 DITTO
13 DITTO
14 DITTO
15 OFFICE
16 CLEANERS ROOM
17 DITTO
GOODS LIFT
PLENUM
RISING ELECTRICAL DUCT
PRIVATE OFFICE
PRIVATE OFFICE
PRIVATE OFFICE
DITTO

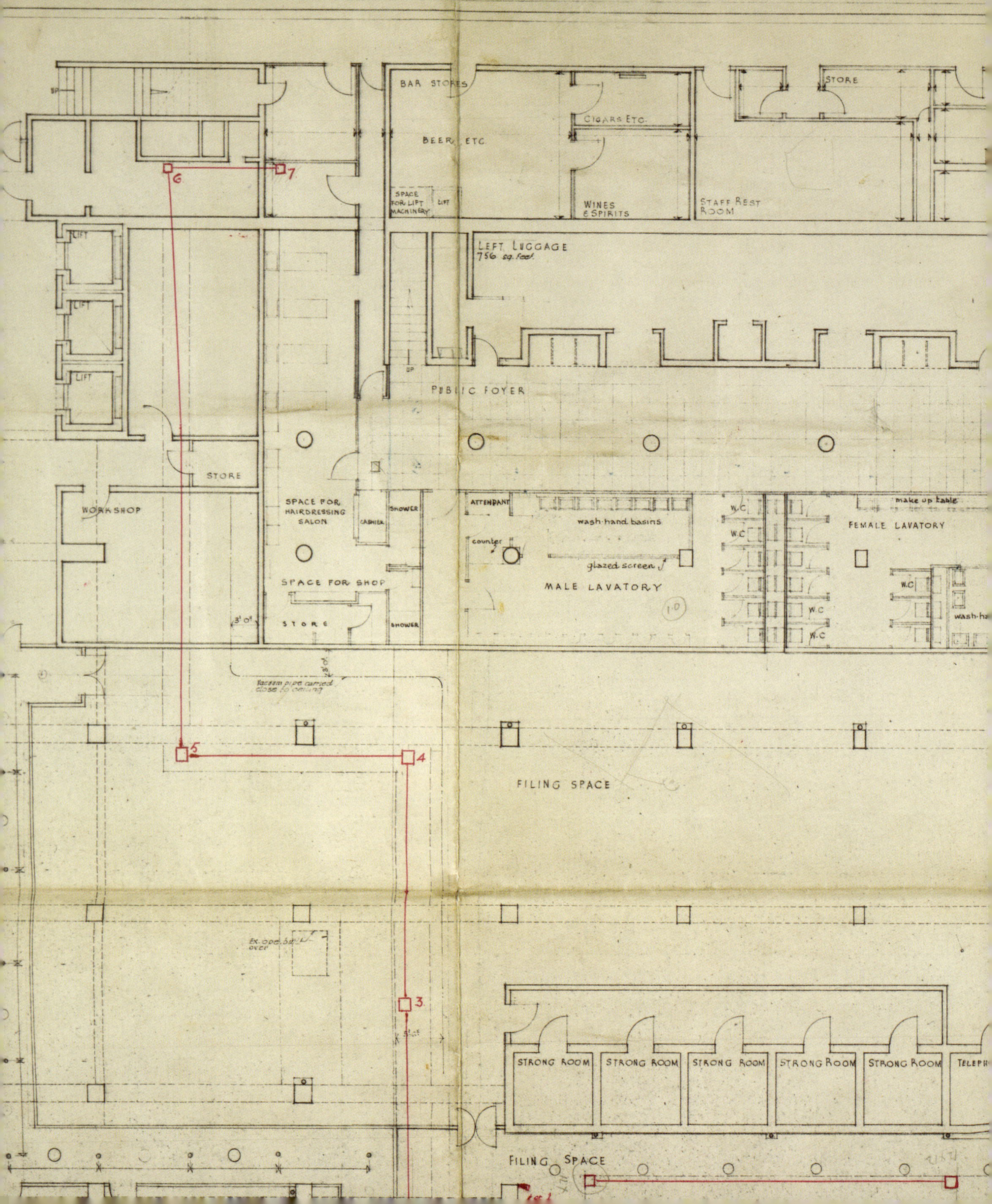

BAR STORES
BEER ETC.
CIGARS ETC.
WINES & SPIRITS
SPACE FOR LIFT MACHINERY
LIFT
STAFF REST ROOM
STORE
LIFT
LIFT
LIFT
LEFT LUGGAGE
756 sq. feet
PUBLIC FOYER
UP
STORE
WORKSHOP
SPACE FOR HAIRDRESSING SALON
CASHIER
SHOWER
SPACE FOR SHOP
STORE
SHOWER
ATTENDANT
wash-hand basins
counter
glazed screen
MALE LAVATORY
W.C
W.C
W.C
W.C
make up table
FEMALE LAVATORY
W.C
wash-h
FILING SPACE
STRONG ROOM
STRONG ROOM
STRONG ROOM
STRONG ROOM
STRONG ROOM
TELEPH
FILING SPACE
1
2
3
4
5
6
7

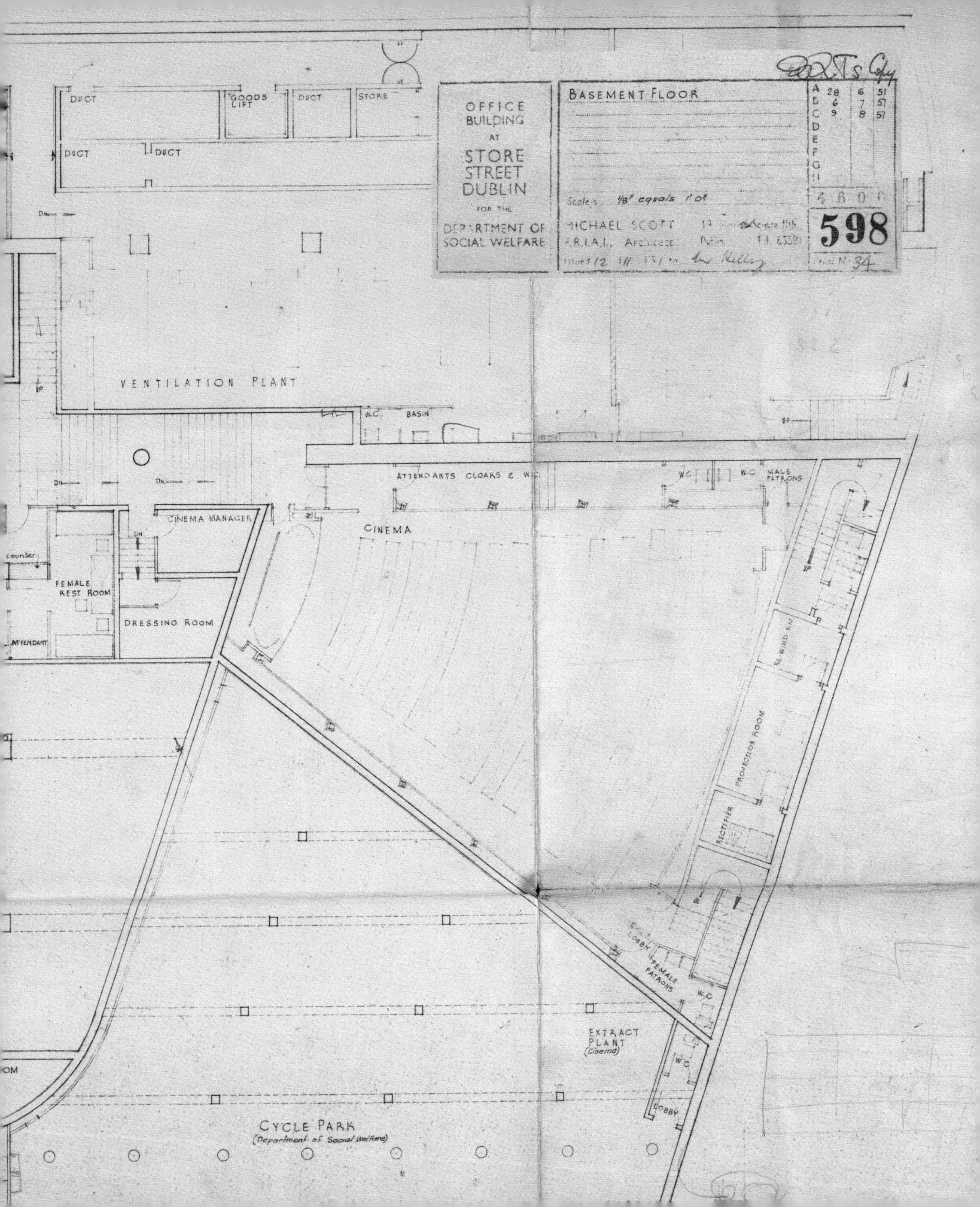
OFFICE
BUILDING
AT
STORE
STREET
DUBLIN
FOR THE
DEPARTMENT OF
SOCIAL WELFARE
BASEMENT FLOOR
Scale 1/8" equals 1' 0"
MICHAEL SCOTT
F.R.I.A.I., Architect
598
DUCT
GOODS LIFT
DUCT
STORE
DUCT
DUCT
VENTILATION PLANT
W.C.
BASIN
ATTENDANTS CLOAKS & W.C.
W.C.
W.C.
MALE PATRONS
CINEMA MANAGER
CINEMA
counter
FEMALE REST ROOM
DRESSING ROOM
ATTENDANT
RE-WIND RM.
PROJECTION ROOM
RECTIFIER
LOBBY
FEMALE PATRONS
W.C.
EXTRACT PLANT
(Cinema)
W.C.
LOBBY
CYCLE PARK
(Department of Social Welfare)

INTRODUCING
Expressway
THE NEW, EASY WAY TO BOOK AND PLAN YOUR JOURNEYS
ADVANCED BOOKING GUARANTEES YOUR SEAT ON ALL ROUTES

LEE DUNNE'S NEW PLAY
RETURN to The Hill
VINCENT SMITH
Booking Eblana 2pm Daily
Written & Directed by LEE DUNNE

SPRING WATER

BICYCLES MUST BE STACKED
IN THE RACKS PROVIDED

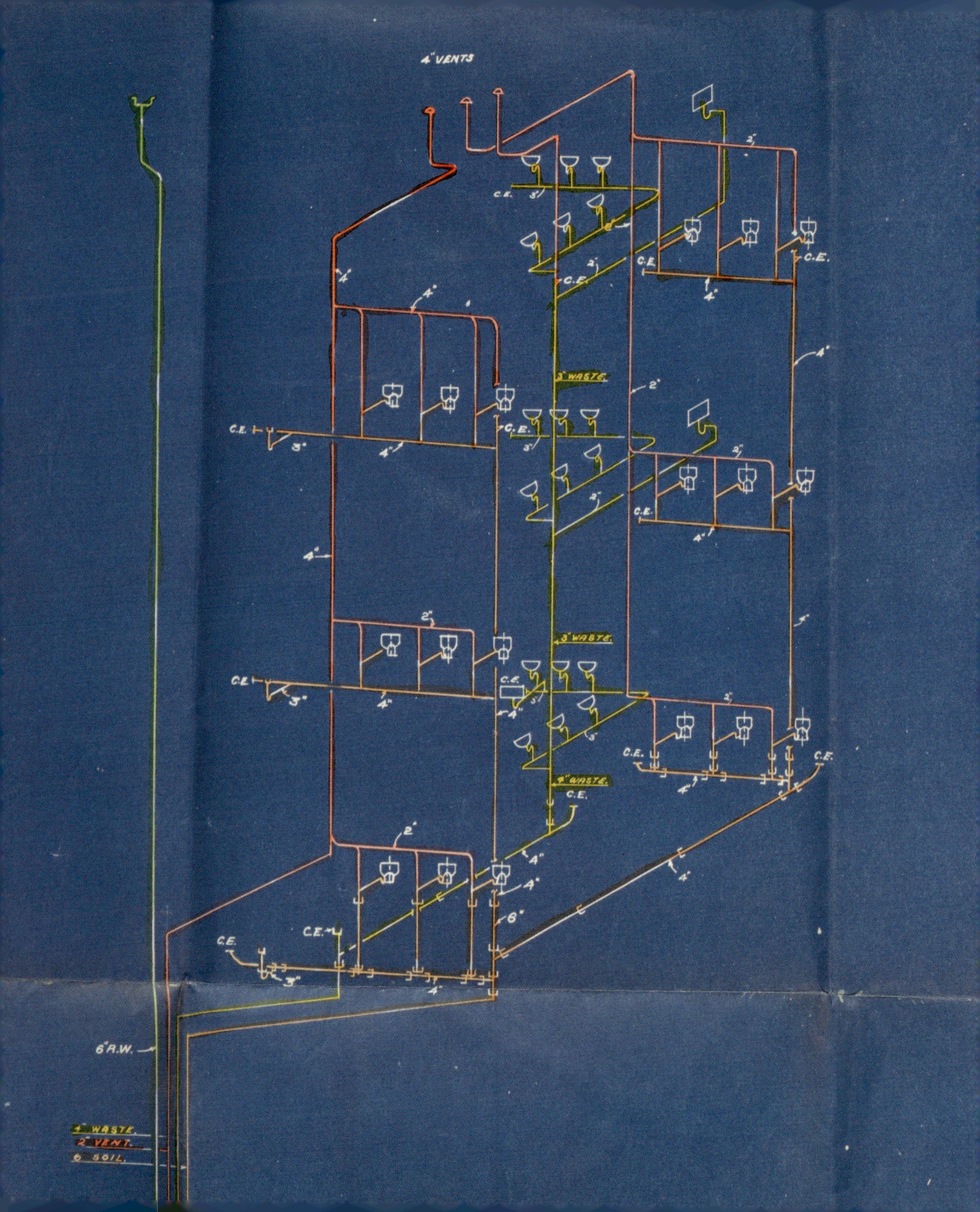
4" VENTS
3" WASTE
3" WASTE
4" WASTE
C.E.
6" R.W.
4" WASTE
2" VENT
6" SOIL

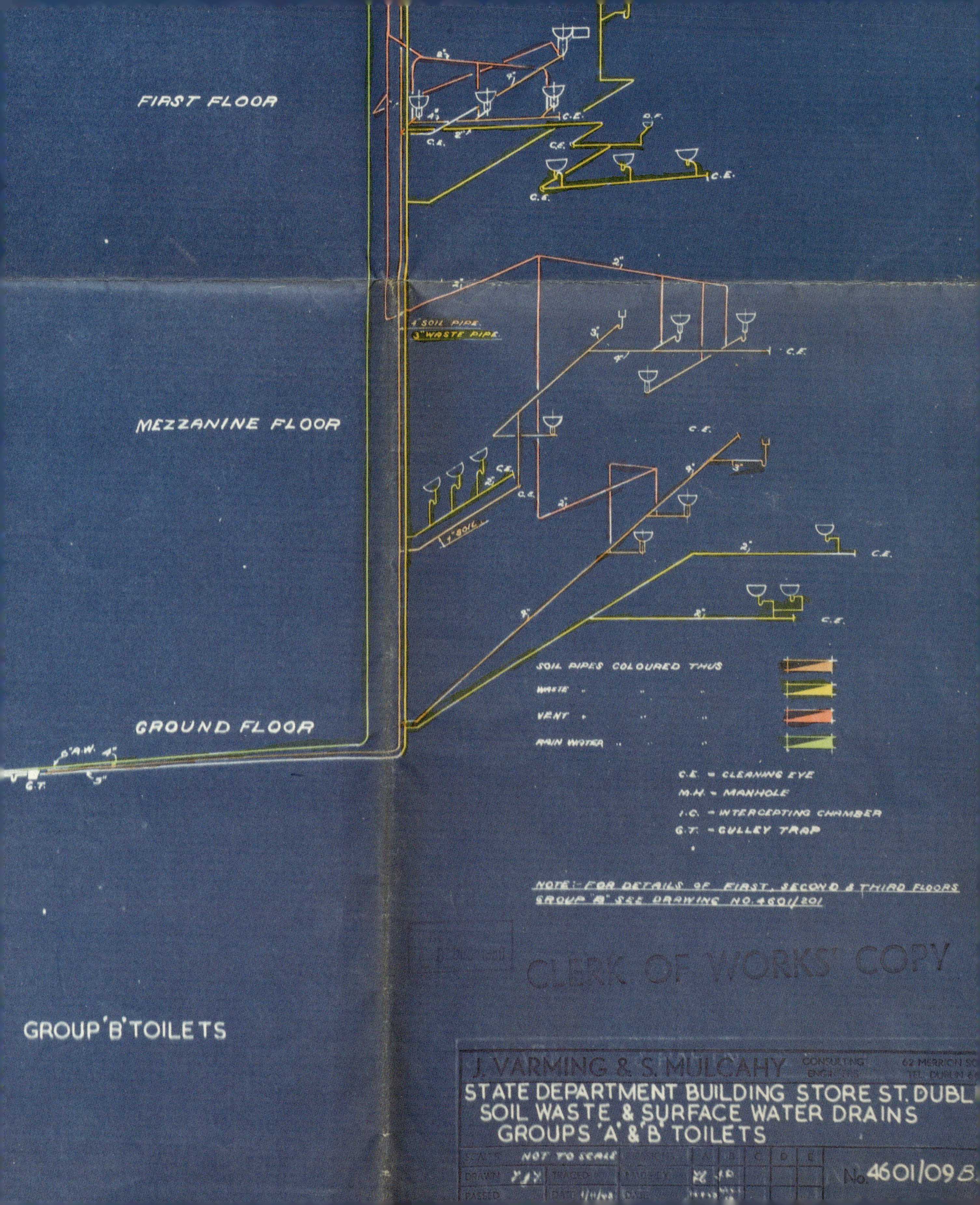

FIRST FLOOR
C.E.
D.F.
MEZZANINE FLOOR
4" SOIL PIPE
3" WASTE PIPE
4" SOIL
GROUND FLOOR
G.T.
SOIL PIPES COLOURED THUS
WASTE
VENT
RAIN WATER
C.E. = CLEANING EYE
M.H. = MANHOLE
I.C. = INTERCEPTING CHAMBER
G.T. = GULLEY TRAP
NOTE:- FOR DETAILS OF FIRST, SECOND & THIRD FLOORS GROUP 'B' SEE DRAWING NO. 4601/201
CLERK OF WORKS' COPY
GROUP 'B' TOILETS
J. VARMING & S. MULCAHY
CONSULTING ENGINEERS
STATE DEPARTMENT BUILDING STORE ST. DUBL
SOIL WASTE & SURFACE WATER DRAINS
GROUPS 'A' & 'B' TOILETS
NOT TO SCALE
No. 4601/09 B

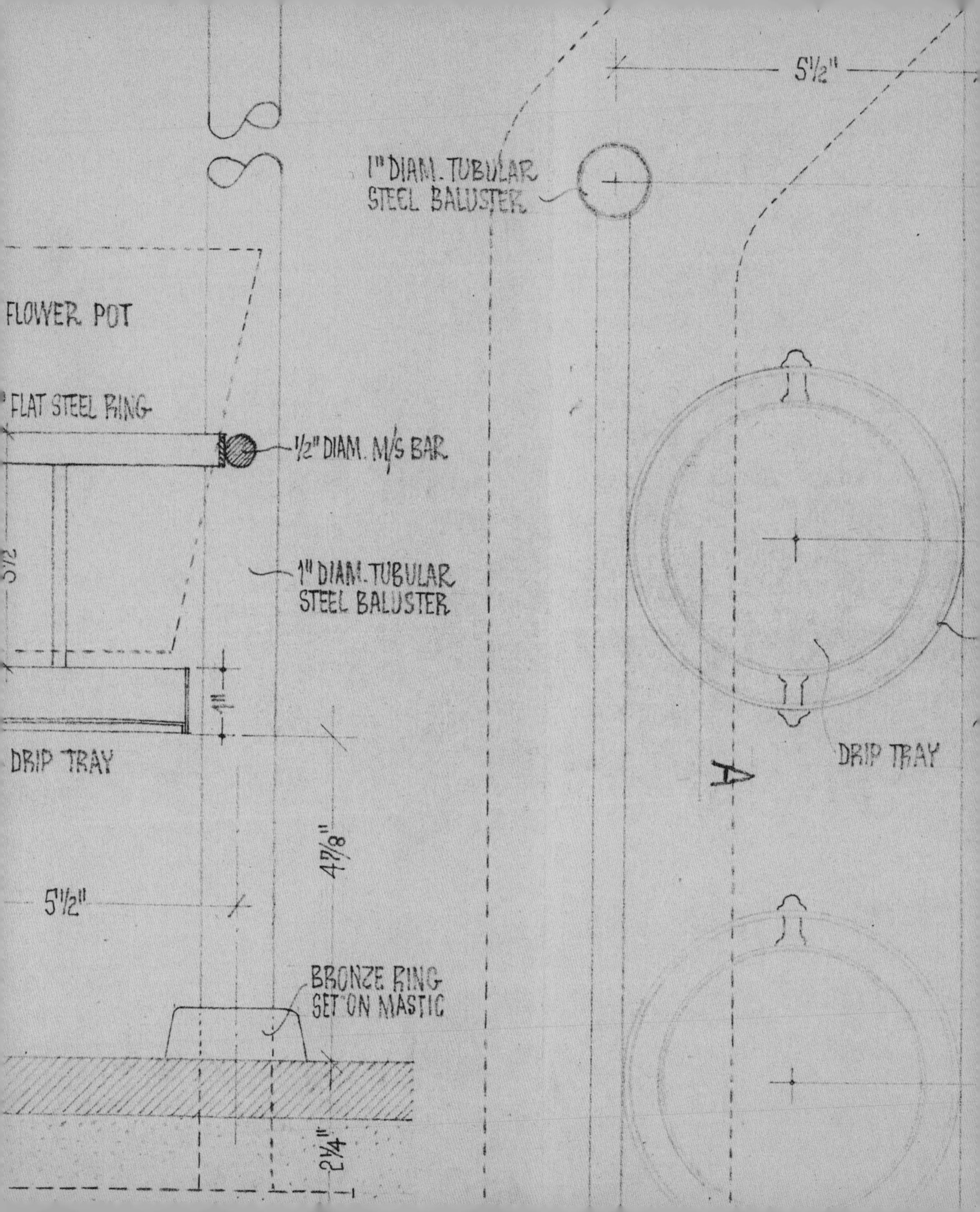
5½"
1" DIAM. TUBULAR STEEL BALUSTER
FLOWER POT
FLAT STEEL RING
½" DIAM. M/S BAR
1" DIAM. TUBULAR STEEL BALUSTER
1"
DRIP TRAY
DRIP TRAY
A
4⅞"
5½"
BRONZE RING SET ON MASTIC
2¼"

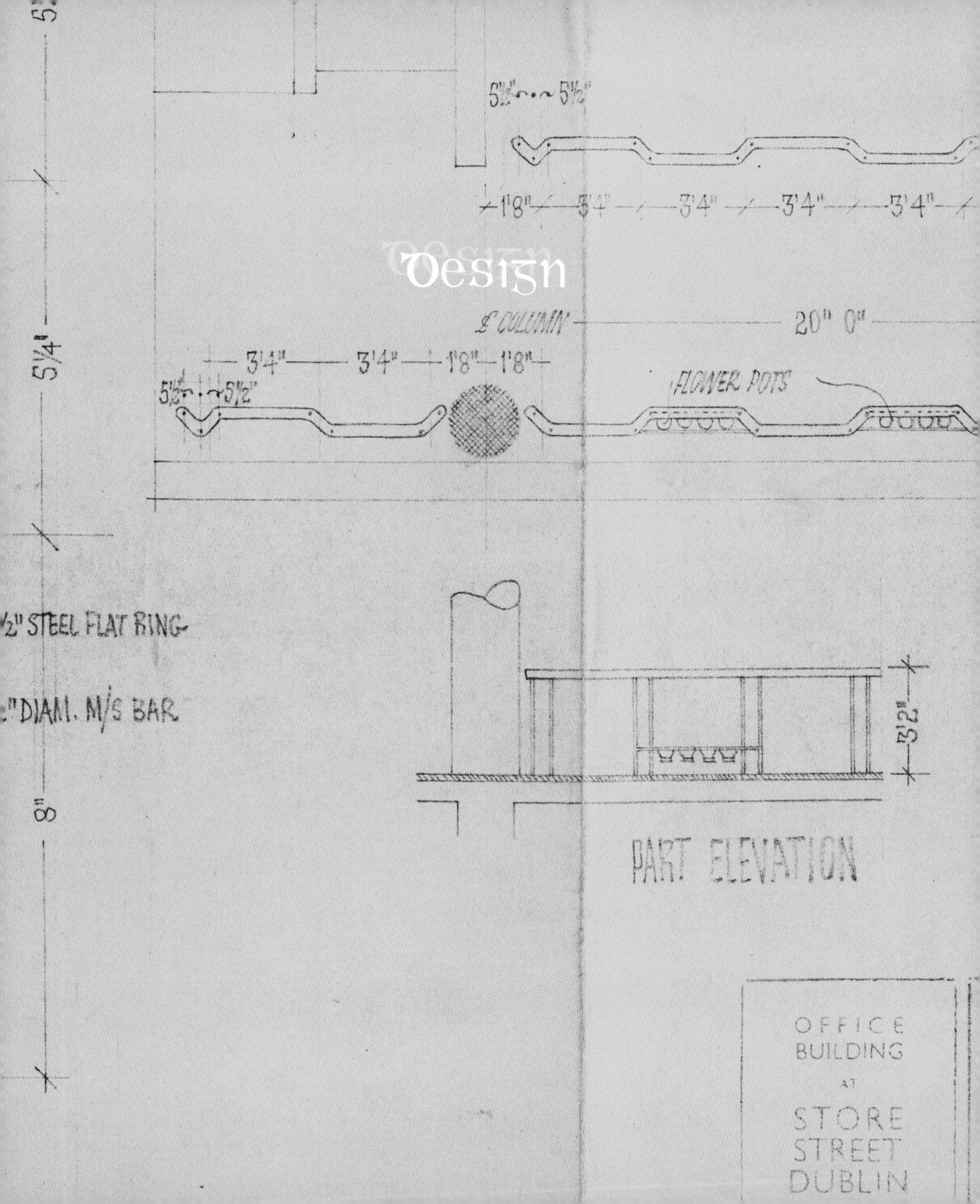
5½" ~ 5½"
1'8" 3'4" 3'4" 3'4" 3'4"
℄ COLUMN
20' 0"
3'4" 3'4" 1'8" 1'8"
5½" ~ 5½"
FLOWER POTS
5'4"
½" STEEL FLAT RING
"DIAM. M/S BAR
3'2"
8"
PART ELEVATION
OFFICE
BUILDING
AT
STORE
STREET
DUBLIN

Design

Our ultimate goal, therefore, was the composite but inseparable work of art, the great building, in which the old dividing line between monumental and decorative elements would have disappeared for ever.

Walter Gropius

Michael Scott and Art

Throughout his life, Michael Scott had a passion for the arts. From his training in the Metropolitan School of Art as a young man to his key part in the seminal Rosc modern art exhibitions from the 1960s, art played a central role in his work. More than this, the decorative arts – and craft more generally – were integral to his architecture.

Paul Clerkin argues that Scott 'saw architecture as more than just the provision of a building's fabric' and that architects 'should always try to incorporate works of art into their buildings'.[1] Scott included the use of murals in his early hospital commissions during the 1930s.[2] Material historian Lisa Godson argues that this approach was widespread in avant-garde European architectural circles at the time, where 'creating buildings in which art and architecture would be integrated is central to a lot of post 1930s modernism'.[3]

The influence of American modernist architect Frank Lloyd Wright, as well as Europeans like Walter Gropius and Le Corbusier, are evident here in that all three integrated craft and design into their architecture.

An instructive example is the Bauhaus college Sommerfeld House project, designed by Gropius and his students. MacCarthy describes it

as ‘a visionary building, developed as a truly collaborative work’ in which students and teachers crafted ‘coloured glass windows, sculptural reliefs in wood, metal screens and lighting fixtures’ within the Berlin house during the 1920s.[4]

This approach was central to Scott’s vision for Áras Mhic Dhiarmada and Busáras. Every element of the building, from the artwork on the ceilings, floors and columns, to the design of the furniture and the crafting of the handrails and radiators, was considered an integral element of the overall project.

Scott’s Design Team

In addition to talented architects and engineers, Scott gathered an impressive array of design talent. While all training as architects, a number went on to become Ireland’s leading art practitioners in later years.

Chief among these was Patrick Scott. A trained and practising architect, Scott was a key figure in the avant-garde art movement from the 1940s, actively involved in the White Stag group of painters and sculptors and a member of the Irish Exhibition of Living Art. In later years, Scott would immerse himself full-time in his painting. In 1960, he represented Ireland at the Venice Biennale and won the National Prize at the Guggenheim International Exhibition. Major retrospectives of his work were held in Dublin in 1982, 2002 and 2014. He was awarded the highest artistic award in Ireland in 2007 when he was appointed a Saoi of Aosdána.

An early exponent of pure abstraction in his visual art, Scott was principally responsible for the glass-tile mosaic murals on the balcony of the sixth-floor restaurant and in the ministerial corridor at Busáras.

Scott was joined by sculptor Barney Heron. Brother of the better-known sculptor Hilary Heron, Barney specialised in timber and metal work, the design of which Clerkin acknowledges as ‘innovative pre-fabricated structures’, including the mezzanine restaurant radiators that doubled as guard rails for the floor-to-ceiling glass windows on the building’s north face.[5]

The other outstanding design feature of the building was the bespoke furniture in the concourse, restaurants and offices designed by Robin Walker. Walker had studied under Le Corbusier before joining Scott, and later in his career worked with other leading modernist architects, including Mies van der Rohe. Walker is recognised today as one of Ireland's leading modernist architects, and his impressive body of work included the 1961 Bord Fáilte building in Dublin (now demolished), as well as a number of key buildings on the UCD campus in Belfield and the Bothar Buí artists' retreat in County Cork.

The work of these three men added significantly to the modern look and feel of Busáras, bringing colour, comfort and innovation to the interior of both the bus station and the departmental offices.

The Festival of Britain

While much of the theory behind combining arts, craft and architecture at Áras Mhic Dhiarmada and Busáras came from continental European and American sources, its specific aesthetic owed more to Scandinavian influences. This was in part the result of the architects going on study trips to countries such as Finland in the 1930s, but the style gained greater strength after they attended the Festival of Britain in 1951.

The Festival of Britain was 'a commercial and cultural showcase for the promotion of trade and the education of the people'.[6] For its main organiser, journalist and publisher Gerald Barry, it was to be 'a popular demonstration of national renewal'.[7]

The festival was in the tradition of the Great Exhibition held in London's Crystal Palace in the nineteenth century, intended to showcase the very best of modern British industry and design. Actively

supported by the post-war British Labour Party government, the series of exhibitions in London and other regional capitals was more than just a showcase; it was an attempt to define a modern mid-century British cultural identity. In doing so, it provided opportunities for a young generation of artists, designers and architects to showcase their interpretation of that culture. Historian of the festival Barry Turner described this dimension of the event as 'a propaganda exercise, a concerted attempt by mostly young designers to show that their alternative to conventional taste would make happier lives'.[8]

Like their Irish counterparts working on Busáras at the time, this younger generation in London was influenced by Le Corbusier, Bauhaus and other icons of Continental European and American modernism. However, Turner rightly argues that 'in the end, it was Northern Europe that held sway, because it was there in the Nordic democracies that modern design was combined with a social message that had a strong appeal to those who looked to a more egalitarian society'.[9]

The proximity of this key cultural event in London, coming just as construction and the fitting out of Áras Mhic Dhiarmada and Busáras had recommenced, cemented an already present Scandinavian influence within Michael Scott's design team.

Both O'Connor and Godson stress the importance of both the Scandinavian influence and the Festival of Britain when it came to deciding the final colour, design and material choice at Busáras.[10]

Modern Irish architects and designers were attracted to the warmer and more human finish of Scandinavian modernism than the, at times, austere approach popular on the Continent. Likewise, in Britain a continuity was drawn from the nineteenth-century Arts and Crafts movement to the mid-century modern moment, which, while stylistically different, emphasised the democratising nature of architecture and design, and its capacity to improve people's lives.

In Ireland there was also an identification with both the existing craft traditions of countries like Denmark and Finland, as well as their small-country status. This lent itself to a more nuanced approach to combining traditional and modern materials, styles and methods, giving Áras Mhic Dhiarmada, like its Scandinavian and British counterparts, a distinctively vernacular feel.

Materials

All of these approaches are evident in the wide range of materials used in Áras Mhic Dhiarmada. Scott stressed the need to use quality materials, whether they hailed from Ireland or abroad. While the ever-imposing constraints of finance, particularly during the final battles with Secretary General Dan O'Donovan, had an impact, even here some important innovations were secured.

The exterior of the building is predominantly made up of fine Portland stone and handmade flat Kingscourt brick from Co. Cavan. The interior of the building includes finely polished green Connemara marble casing on the Áras Mhic Dhiarmada stairwell. The way in which the Portland stone references the neighbouring Custom House has already been noted. A similar effect is also achieved by the use of copper

on the metalwork along the south-facing third- and sixth-floor balconies, mirroring the oxidised green copper dome on Gandon's eighteenth-century masterpiece.

A wide range of timbers was used in the furniture, office panelling, concourse kiosks and handrails, including Irish oak, African mahogany, Siamese teak and Canadian maple. For Godson, it is the 'really fine detailing' that stands out as much as the materials themselves.[11]

Niall Scott also emphasised the quality of the materials and the 'elegance' of the design, complimenting 'how beautifully it was put together'.[12] O'Connor compared the use of materials to the 'artisan quality of design' in Danish modernism during the same period, while Rowley stressed how the combination of high-quality materials, particularly in many of the public spaces of the building, gave it a 'luxurious' quality.[13] For Clerkin, 'All of these materials and more combine to give Busáras an opulence that is in contrast to the simple forms of the furniture and building.'[14]

Mosaics

The most distinctive interior feature of both the bus station and Department of Social Protection is the widespread use of glass mosaic tiling in the terrazzo floors, support columns and third- and sixth-floor offices and restaurant.

The tiles were sourced by Scott from SAIRM in Venice and had a dual function, being both aesthetically pleasing and practical to maintain. The colour scheme throughout the building added to the warmer tone of much of the design and materials.

The concourse glass tiling is predominantly green-and-white and red-and-white square tiles, with a similar colour scheme in the basement.

The exterior of the bus control tower in composed of blue tiles in diagonal bands broken with blue triangles. The ministerial corridor on the third floor also uses blue tiles for the interior of the offices, and a red-and-white candy-stripe pattern for the balcony corridors.

The sixth-floor restaurant has solid red tiled columns and conical skylights tiled in bright yellow. The red tile is then repeated on the outside of the skylights on the roof.

However, the standout use of mosaic is on the canopies of the sixth-floor balconies. Overlooking Store Street to the west is the large fin-tail canopy with a simple series of diamond or leaf-shaped abstract shapes. These are set in red, yellow and blue against a white-tiled background. A similar colour scheme is used for the smaller canopies on the south-facing balcony, in a series of monochrome mosaics with more organic abstract leaf shapes.

While today these mosaics are only visible to the public from street level, the attention to colour and detail on the sixth floor was originally intended for the public. In an interview with Paul Clerkin, Pat Scott emphasises this important point:

> The top floor restaurant was originally meant to be a public space, a restaurant during the day and a night-club in the evening. The lifts would take people from the reception area to the top floor. That explains the colour and details in the restaurant, like the skylight. I just thought as a public space they should be bright and colourful.[15]

In the same interview, Scott also stressed that the designs were purely abstract, 'with no symbolism'. The colour scheme, however, is clearly reflective of the prominence of primary colours in both the painting and design of Theo van Doesburg, the Dutch founder and leader of De Stijl, and the abstract paintings of Henri Matisse. Both artists would have been widely known among the Irish artistic avant-garde at the time, including Scott.

While Scott is unsure whether there was ever a formal plan to have a mosaic under the corrugated concrete canopy, other sources indicate that this proposal, along with a plan to have a Scott tapestry in Áras Mhic Dhiarmada's reception, were vetoed by Dan O'Donovan on financial grounds.

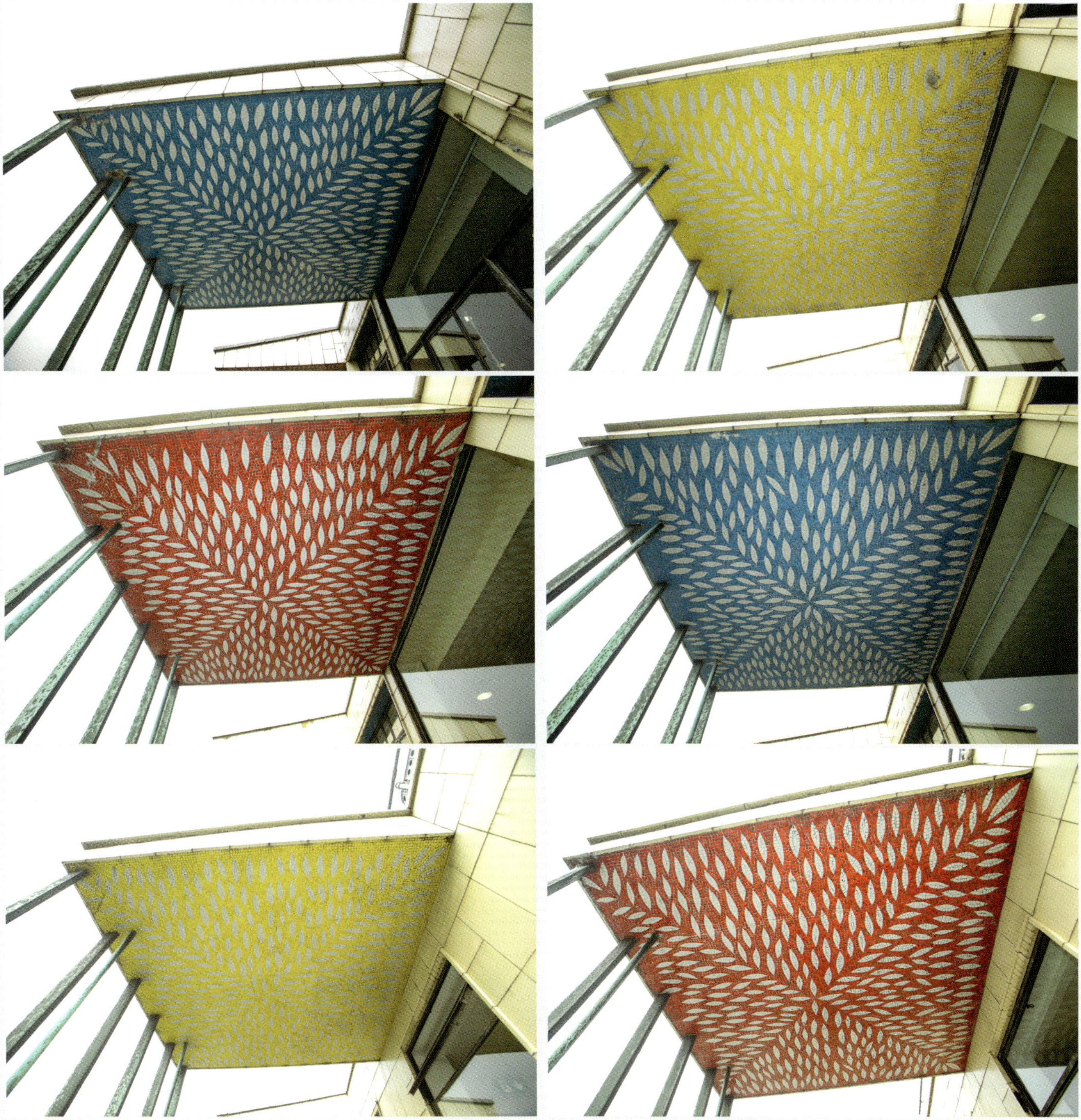

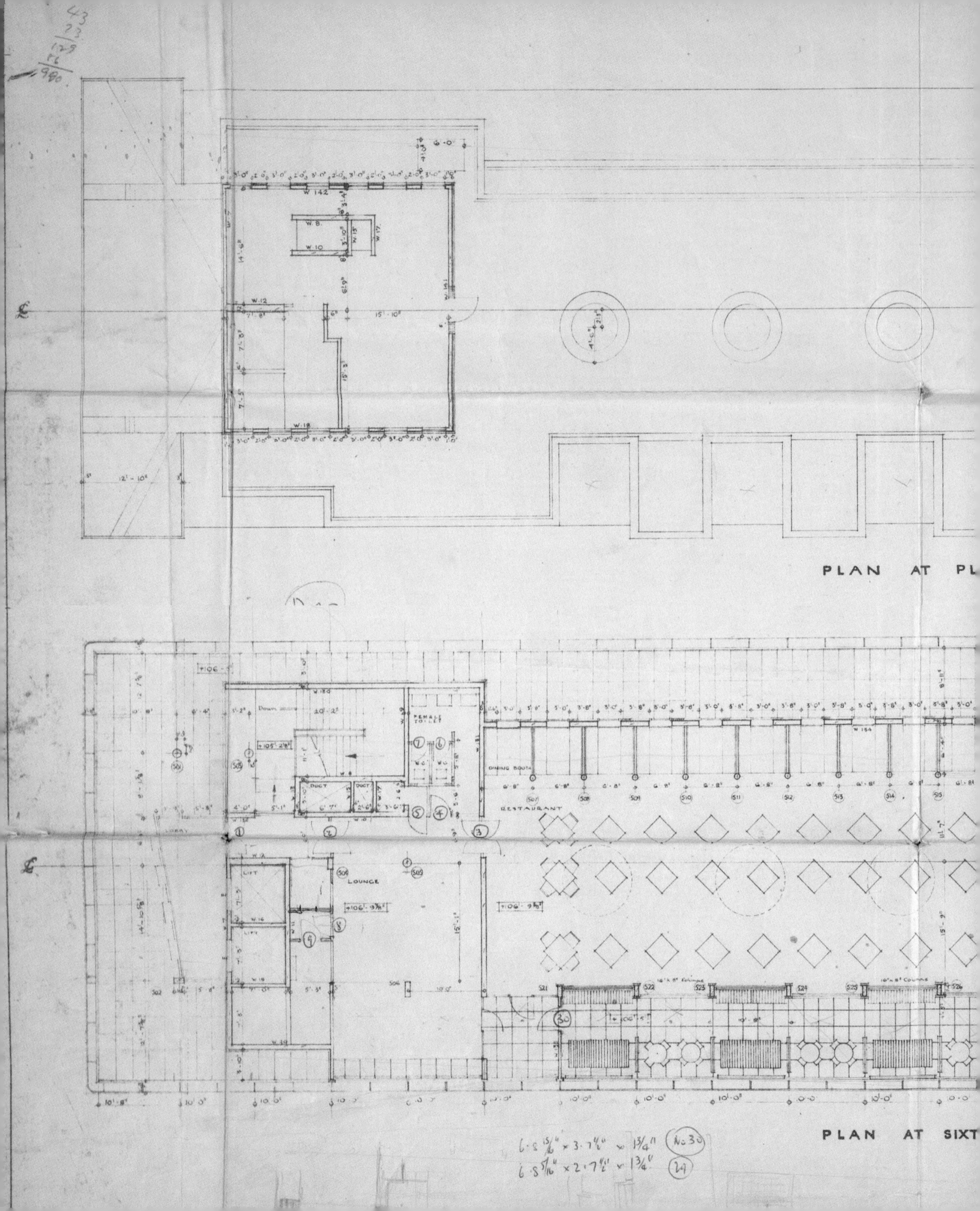
PLAN AT PL
LOUNGE
RESTAURANT
FEMALE TOILET
DINING BOOTH
LIFT
DUCT
PLAN AT SIXT

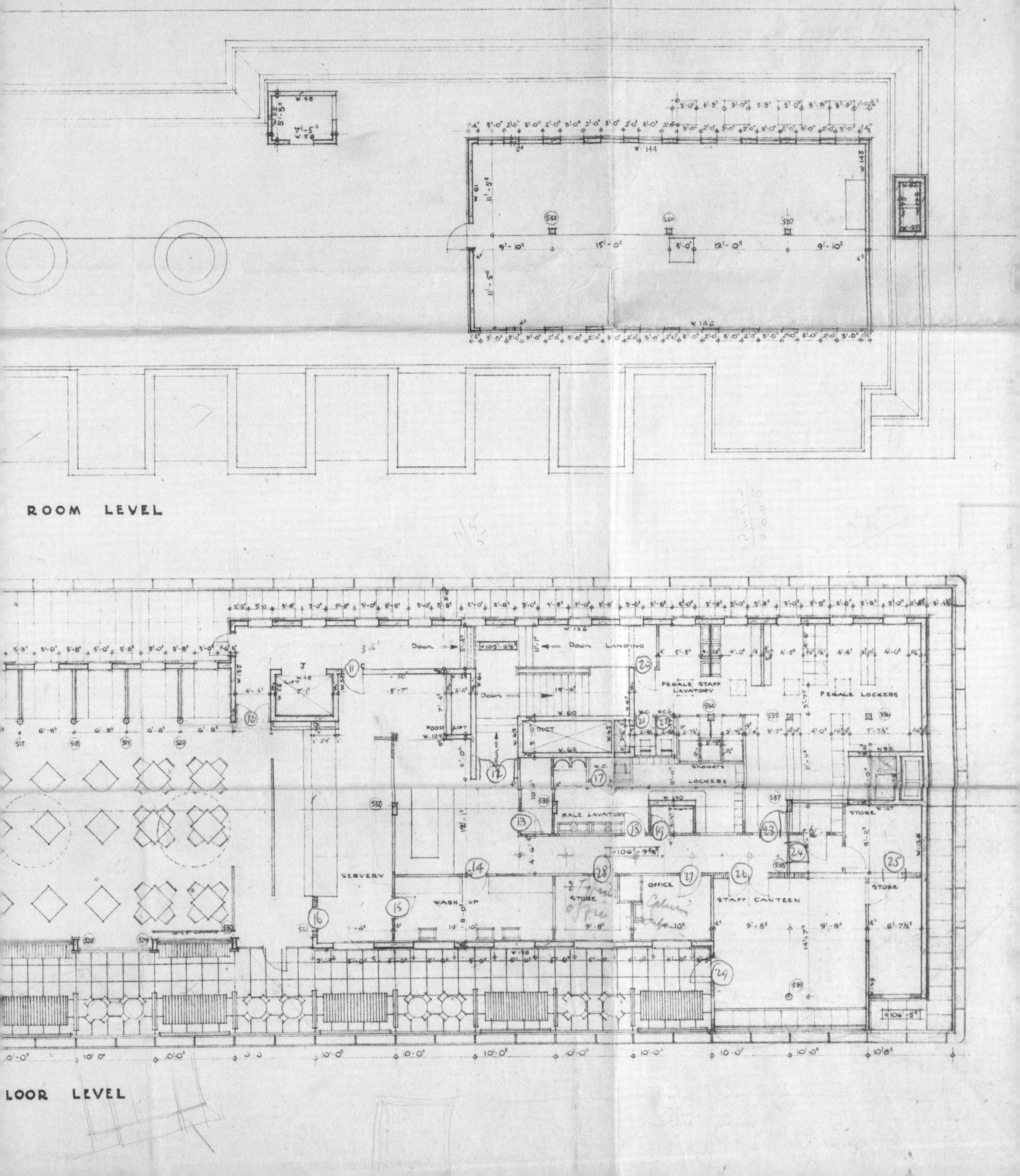
ROOM LEVEL
SERVERY
WASH UP
STORE
OFFICE
STAFF CANTEEN
MALE LAVATORY
LOCKERS
SHOWERS
FEMALE STAFF LAVATORY
FEMALE LOCKERS
DUCT
LIFT
FOOD LIFT
LANDING
Down
W.C.
LOOR LEVEL

Furniture and Fittings

While none of the original furniture of Busáras survives today, we get a glimpse of its design from Richard Deegan's contemporary photographs in Basil Clancy's 1954 monograph on the building.[16] The forty-nine black-and-white photographs display a sharp, clean, modern building whose exterior is made up of straight lines at right angles. In contrast, the interior – and in particular the furniture and fittings – are curved and soft, again emphasising the Scandinavian and Festival of Britain influences.

The concourse wooden seating with fitted waste bins ensured the waiting area was uncluttered yet comfortable. The beech-and-leather restaurant seats and tables are of typical mid-century modern design, combining elegance, simplicity and comfort. The light fittings in the sixth-floor restaurant and basement cinema have a strongly Scandinavian feel, although the latter are almost Art Deco in design, while the former are more modern.

URLÁR A hAOIN

URLÁR 4

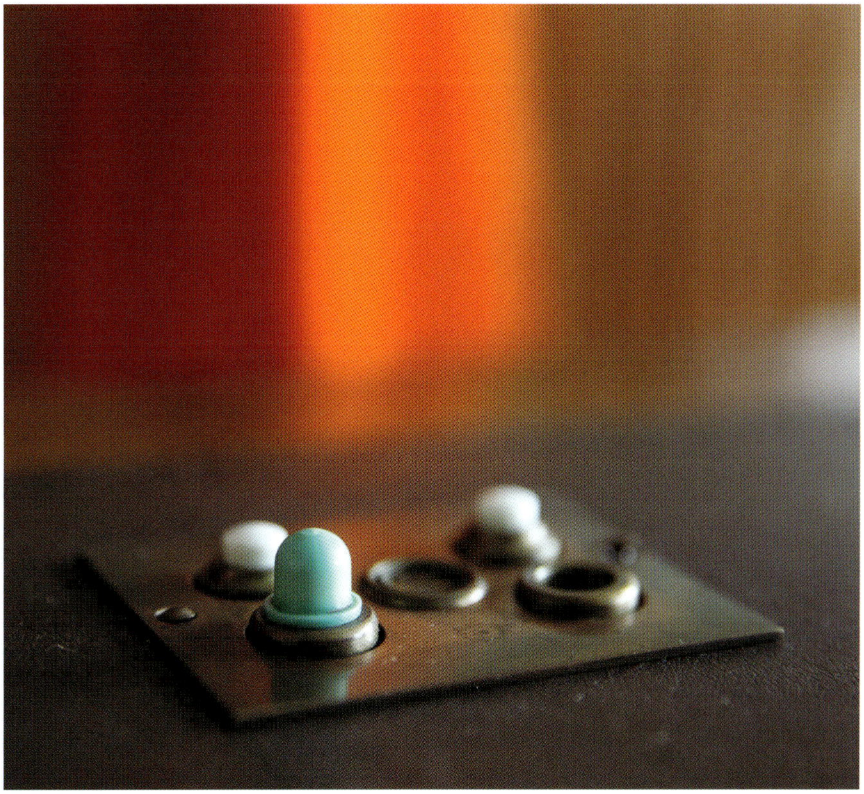

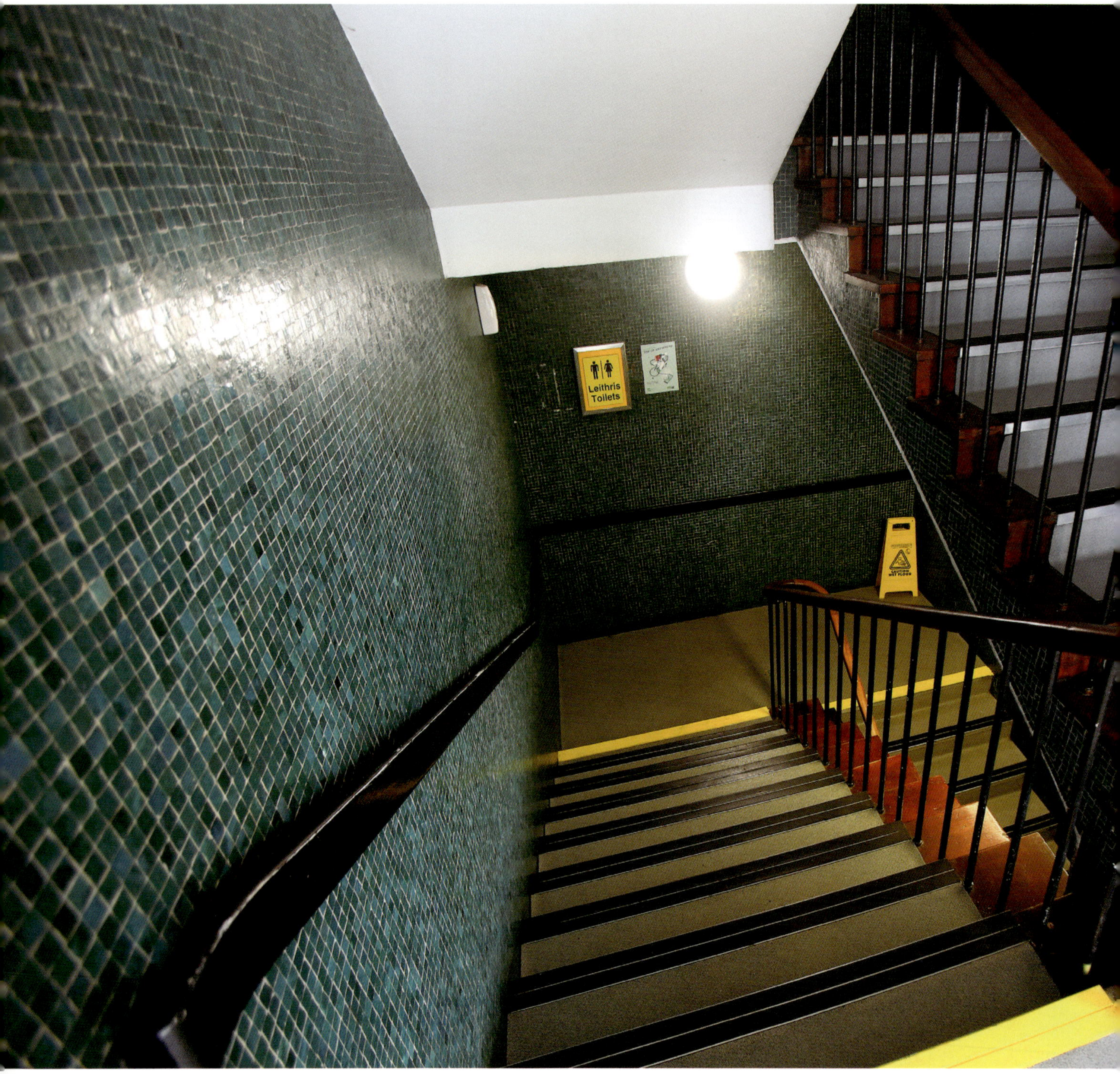
Leithris
Toilets

Lisa Godson suggests that while such modern furniture was not unknown in Ireland at the time, it would not have been found in people's homes. Rather, such modern fittings would only be found in 'sites of fantasy and leisure like theatres, cinemas and ice cream parlours'. She makes the case that 'the glamour of air travel is borrowed by bus travel', thus giving ordinary people daily access to a style and level of comfort usually reserved for the realms of entertainment or luxury travel.[17]

Assessment

Paul Clerkin argues that Michael Scott's use of materials in Busáras was evidence of a belief that 'traditional and modern materials could all be used harmoniously in a modern way'.[18] That high-quality materials and contemporary design were given such prominence in a bus station for 'the masses' was, for Clerkin, a demonstration of an 'egalitarianism' at the heart of the entire project.[19]

For Godson, this 'attentiveness to a public space' is indicative of a modernist approach to architecture that sees 'the public as the most significant client'.[20] There is a commitment in the building and, crucially, in its attention to quality design for the materials, furniture and fittings that reflects 'a commitment to celebrating every day activities' and 'democratising access to design'.[21]

In Áras Mhic Dhiarmada, Michael Scott and his team of designers achieved Gropius' objective of erasing the distinction between the monumental and decorative. That they did this in a building for the general public, and whose most important artistic and design elements were intentionally placed in what were to be the most public of areas, was a tribute to what Godson called 'the dignity of everyday life'.[22]

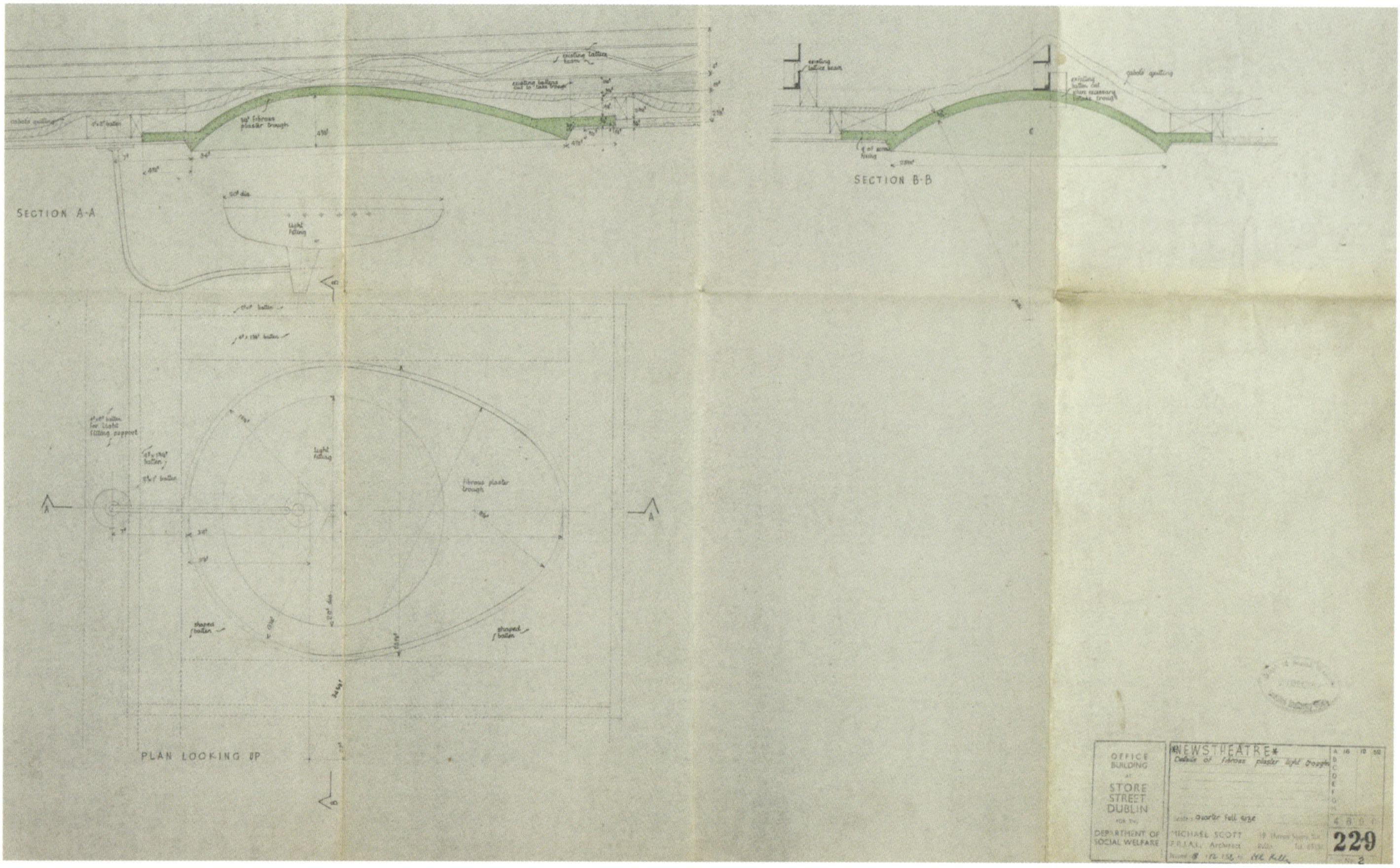
SECTION A-A
SECTION B-B
PLAN LOOKING UP
OFFICE BUILDING AT STORE STREET DUBLIN FOR THE DEPARTMENT OF SOCIAL WELFARE
NEWSTHEATRE
MICHAEL SCOTT
229

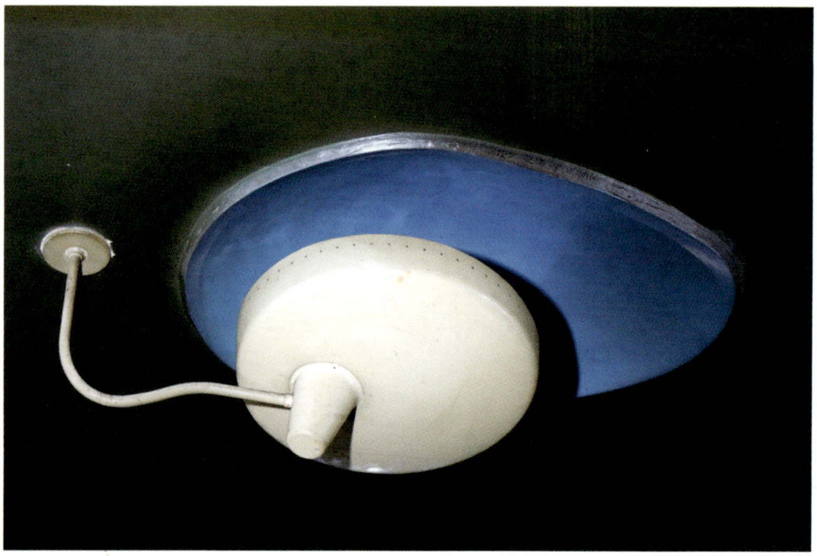

WE NEED TO...
SILENCE
STIFLE
SUPPRESS
CURB
GAG
HUSH
INHIBIT
MUFFLE
MUTE
QUELL
QUIET
REPRESS
RESTRAIN
SQUELCH
STILL
SUBDUE
THROTTLE
TONE DOWN
SILENCE
...IT!

NIGHTLY AT 8pm
EBLANA

A

01
02

people

05
06
TFI

People

Adrian O'Loughlin
42
Regional Operations Manager East for Bus Éireann
From: Portlaoise, Co. Laois
Lives: Swords, Co. Dublin

What is your connection with the building?
In 2000, I started in the ticket office as a junior clerk. I spent two or three years in there. Then I took charge of overall office operations. I was then in charge of private operations within the building. Five years ago, I became regional operations manager, as well as having responsibility for the building.

What do you think of the building?
I'm very proud of the building. When I first came in, I didn't realise what we had. As I developed through my career, I became more appreciative, more understanding.

What feature of the building stands out for you?
You're always struck by the columns when you walk into the building. But the wow factor for me is the Eblana Theatre. It's just such a hidden gem.

Do you know much about the building's history?
I've got to learn a bit as I've developed my career here. It's a fascinating story of the building, its conception, its origin, how it was developed. It divided a lot of opinion at the time, in terms of its location, its scale and costs.

What is your first memory of the building?
I was here when I was eighteen, as a passenger. To me it was just a big building. It didn't make any impression on me at that time.

What is your most important memory of the building?
For me, it's the people that make the building. And I've been lucky enough to work with some real characters. We've had people who worked here for forty-one years, twenty years. Porters, supervisors, drivers, ancillary staff, cleaners, security. Amazing characters have come through the building.

What do you think should happen to the building?
It should be showcased for what it is. It is more than a just a bus station. People who come in and out are only familiar with what happens on the floor. It would be great to see more life back in the building.

"I'm very proud of the building. When I first came in, I didn't realise what we had. As I developed through my career, I became more appreciative, more understanding.

05
06
Bus Éireann

Rhonda Byrne
49
Bus driver
From: Dublin
Lives in: Kells, Co. Meath

What is your connection to the building?
I'm a bus driver. I was an acting supervisor, working in the bus station daily. I'm fourteen years with Bus Éireann. When I started, I was all over the country, but for the last ten years I'm on the 109, which would be Kells to Dublin, or the 109a which is Kells to Dublin Airport.

What feature of the building stands out for you?
The canopy outside. I love that. And the pillars, the mosaic tiles on them are just fabulous. You look at the International Financial Services Centre building, it's boring. There's nothing interesting about it. The Custom House has been done up and is lovely. But to me, Busáras just stands out.

Do you know much about the building's history?
I've learned a bit, the four different sites, they paid £13,000 for the site, the back and forward with the government, it took so long with the construction from the 1940s to the 1950s.

"You think about all the people that would have travelled from the country up to work in Dublin, young girls and boys only starting out, and the nerves.

What is your first memory of the building?
Probably as a new driver coming in and going, wow! Then it was Aidan, Mr Busáras. I remember when I came in as an acting inspector, I had known Aidan, he was just a fountain of knowledge. I remember the first day I was here saying, 'Now, Aidan, you're going to mind me,' and he says, 'Don't worry, I'm going to mind you.' Everybody knew him. For me, he would be the standard.

Any other stand-out memories of the building?
There's lots, you're meeting so many different people and you're hearing so many different stories. I was standing here this morning and picturing the bus station fifty years ago, picturing it in black and white. You think about all the people that would have travelled from the country up to work in Dublin, young girls and boys only starting out, and the nerves.

What should happen to the building?
It definitely should be restored to its former glory, that would be fabulous.

02
03
04
STAYCATION
buseireann.ie
4

Arturas Danaitis

37
Bus station supervisor
From: Russia
Living in: Co. Wicklow

What is your connection to the building?
I first came here seven years ago. I remember when I saw the building for the first time, it was an amazing building for me. I came from a post-Soviet Union country, and back then everything was grey. And then you come here, you say, whoa, it's amazing.

Do you remember the first time you were in the building?
I was going to Dungannon and I came from Ferns to get a connection to Monaghan. It was dark outside. We were going to visit our friends from Russia. I was very scared and shaking because it was so busy, so many people and I didn't know much English.

What do you think of the building?
I love the building, it's amazing. It has a theatre downstairs, it has another two floors under the theatre for the big pumps to soak the water back to the Liffey. It had a restaurant on the second floor. It was one of only two places in Dublin where you could get a pint on Christmas Day: Connolly and Busáras, once you bought the ticket. It was the first building of the new style after the Second World War.

"I remember when I saw the building for the first time, it was an amazing building for me.

People

BUS ÉIREANN
ROAD PASSENGER SERVICES

What feature of the building stands out for you?
Probably that green sign with the red dog when you're coming in.

Any other interesting stories from your time here?
A couple of stories from the old drivers, like when the buses were parking backwards, if the drivers opened the doors the bus station would fill up with smoke.

What should happen to the building?
It should be a museum and a main point of departure for all tours of Dublin. They should restore the second floor to be a restaurant, make a real proper museum for people who come to Ireland and even for the Irish people to remind them what it was back then in the 1960s.

> "I love the building, it's amazing. It has a theatre downstairs, it has another two floors under the theatre ... It should be a museum and a main point of departure for all tours of Dublin ... for people who come to Ireland and even for the Irish people to remind them what it was back then in the 1960s.

Aisling Clarke
48
Clerical Officer, Department of Social Protection
From: Artane, Dublin
Lives in: Clonsilla, Dublin

"

... the canteen which overlooks the River Liffey and the Custom House. There are amazing views of the city which also include the Dublin mountains in the distance.

What's your connection with the building?
I've worked in Áras Mhic Dhiarmada since 1995. I was assigned to the planning section as a clerical assistant (typist) for a number of years. I also worked in the budget section. For the past fifteen years, I have worked in the secretary general's office. Both my parents also worked in the building. My mam worked in the children's allowance section from 1962 to 1968. My dad worked in the occupational injury benefit from 1978 to 1981.

What feature of the building most stands out?
For me, it's the canteen which overlooks the River Liffey and the Custom House. There are amazing views of the city which also include the Dublin mountains in the distance.

What do you think of the building?
From the outside, you look at it and you're not really impressed. But then when you go inside, it has many outstanding features such as the mosaic tiles and terrazzo stairways.

What is your favourite memory from the building?
In May 2016, the Department organised a 1916 centenary event to honour the memory of Seán Mac Diarmada, the building's namesake. It was a lovely evening with staff and family and friends of Mac Diarmada.

What do you think should happen to the building?
Maybe the Eblana Theatre could re-open as a concert or recital venue and incorporate the sixth-floor canteen as a pop-up restaurant for a full night of entertainment in the building.

Greg Simons
52
Estate Management, Department of Social Protection
From: London
Lives in: Skerries, Co. Dublin

What's your connection to the building?
Estate management means looking after all the Intreo offices nationwide for social welfare, but also looking after the offices in Dublin, including where we are now. I spend an awful lot of time in the basement here dealing with leaks, floods, fire alarms, furniture requests, rodents. You name it, I deal with it.

What feature of the building stands out for you?
Well, where are we standing now in the basement is one of my favourites. It's all dusty and there's lots of little rooms, some of which I've only discovered.

"... the basement is one of my favourites. It's all dusty and there's lots of little rooms, some of which I've only discovered.

EILEEN
NUALA
SANDRA
EOIN
TURN ME OFF
at the end of the day
TO OPEN
PRIVATE
For use of DEPARTMENT
of SOCIAL WELFARE
STAFF ONLY

Any other parts of the building that stand out to you?
The canteen, obviously. On my first day when I came in and I went up I was amazed by the view. I am allowed onto the roof to show contractors around, so you see a different part of Dublin every time you go up there.

What is your first memory of the building?
The first time I was here was lovely, in the reception area and the artwork and the ceilings. And then just getting the lift up to the canteen and walking through the double doors and seeing the pillars and the old pictures of how the canteen used to be and then actually going out onto the balcony surrounding the building and looking out. I wasn't expecting that view.

What do you think of the building?
I love the building. I don't always love my job. But I love the building, just the look of the building, it's not perfect, which I like.

What should happen to the building?
It should definitely be used more. The canteen, we had a music event up there recently. Just the public coming up to the canteen. We're using it for Open House tours. Give it a sort of special status, so people talk about it and it's in the public eye.

“I love the building. I don't always love my job. But I love the building, just the look of the building, it's not perfect, which I like.

Mary Cullina

59

Clerical Officer, Department of Social Protection

From: Co. Mayo

Lives in: Clonsilla, Dublin

What is your connection to the building?

I came here in 1991, after Treatment Benefits was being decentralised and all the staff were being redeployed. I opted to come here mainly for its location. It's beside Connolly Station.

What do you think of the building?

I think it's very dated. I think it needs an overhaul. It's a very good location. There seem to be ongoing problems with controlling the heat and ventilation.

Is there any feature of the building that stands out?

I think the view from the canteen, that would be the main one.

Do you remember the first time you were in the building?

No, I don't have any striking memory of the place. I remember when I came into the place first, the desks were old metal desks, it was an open-plan floor. It was very noisy, quite imposing when you walk into it as a new person.

Do you have any stand-out memory of the building?

As Áras Mhic Dhiarmada is the headquarters of the Department, it is frequently shown on news reports involving Social Protection.

What do you think should happen to the building?

It needs an upgrade. About ten years ago, they were talking about moving us down to Smithfield. A lot of people weren't happy because so many people use Connolly Station, so it would have added to people's journeys. It should definitely be maintained, but it does need an upgrade.

Padraig Murray
64
Actor
From: Dublin
Lives in: Dublin

What is your connection with the building?
In the mid- to late-1990s I was involved with Lee Dunne in a production of *Goodbye to the Hill*. It was the longest-running comedy in the history of Irish theatre. When that had all died down, I got a call from Lee saying he was looking to do a sequel called *Return to the Hill*. We did it here in the Eblana around 1995. I played Paddy Maguire in both plays, the main character. It was actually the last show here.

What kind of a theatre venue was the Eblana?
Phillis Ryan and Gemini Productions did a huge number of shows here. There were lots of big productions in the Eblana. When I was a young lad starting off in the industry in Dublin, the Eblana was one of the recognised theatres.

“Phillis Ryan and Gemini Productions did a huge number of shows here. There were lots of big productions in the Eblana. When I was a young lad starting off in the industry in Dublin, the Eblana was one of the recognised theatres.

> "I remember being terrified driving around Busáras because the traffic was always busy with buses and cars competing for road space.

What did you think of the building as a young Dubliner?
Busáras is not somewhere I had ever really been to. I was born in Dublin, my parents were from Dublin, my grandparents on both sides were from Dublin, we never had any country relations.

What's your earliest memory of the building?
My earliest memory is driving along Amiens Street towards it and my father pulling over and saying to me, 'Get in there,' and put me in the driving seat. I was learning at the time. I remember driving and it was really, really busy, and I remember being terrified driving around Busáras because the traffic was always busy with buses and cars competing for road space.

What should happen to the building?
I'd love to see the theatre operating as a theatre again. We don't have a venue of this size, and if we did it would be terribly expensive for a company to hire. I would love Bus Éireann to have a proper theatre administrator to run the place and to offer it to companies. We would have more small-scale theatres in the city centre, which is badly needed.

Rory O'Neill (aka Panti Bliss)
52
Entertainer and publican
From: Ballinrobe, Co. Mayo
Lives in: Dublin

What's your connection to the building?
We didn't have a community school when we finished primary school, so we had to go somewhere else. We were sent to Gormanstown, next-door to my granny's. So I used to get the train three times a year from Mayo to Heuston and come to Busáras to get the bus to Gormanstown. There were rumours that it was dodgy and there was crusiness around the toilets, and so the building to me was always edgy. My first sense that there were queers around was here. It has that exciting, crazy hint of danger about it. It was dark and dingy and thrilling.

What do you think of the building?
I didn't appreciate it at all when I was a teenager. It was just a bus station. I went straight from that school in Gormanstown to art college. My best friend in college, Niall Sweeney, as a Dubliner and a designer, has always been obsessed by Busáras. Architects get Busáras, but the average punter in Dublin does not, so me and Niall used to feel like we were pioneers, having to defend it all the time. One of the reasons why local Dubliners don't appreciate it is because you can't get a good view of it. It's underappreciated because the city itself never gave the people the opportunity to appreciate it.

" There were rumours that it was dodgy ... and so the building to me was always edgy.

Bus Éireann

WE MADE THIS ADVERT
SO YOU WOULD GO
TO OUR WEBSITE!
(THIS ONE)
workshopplay.ie
Exterion
TICKETS
TICKETS
TICKETS
Information
Eolas
Tickets
Ticéid
Eurolines
WC
Toilets
Leithris
Left Luggage
Bagáiste
01
02
03
04
STOP
Bus Éireann

> “I love the mosaics. I’ve always loved the huge, chunky pillars in the concourse. And I love that it’s unashamedly a bus station, the fan quality, I love that it has function over form but that it’s done beautifully.

Is there a feature of the building that stands out?
Obviously, I love the mosaics. I’ve always loved the huge, chunky pillars in the concourse. And I love that it’s unashamedly a bus station, the fan quality, I love that it has function over form but that it’s done beautifully.

What do you think should happen to the building?
I think the building should still be a bus station. It was designed to be a bus station and it’s a very good one, I believe. I wish it was appreciated more. The city should celebrate it more. The outside could do with a lift.

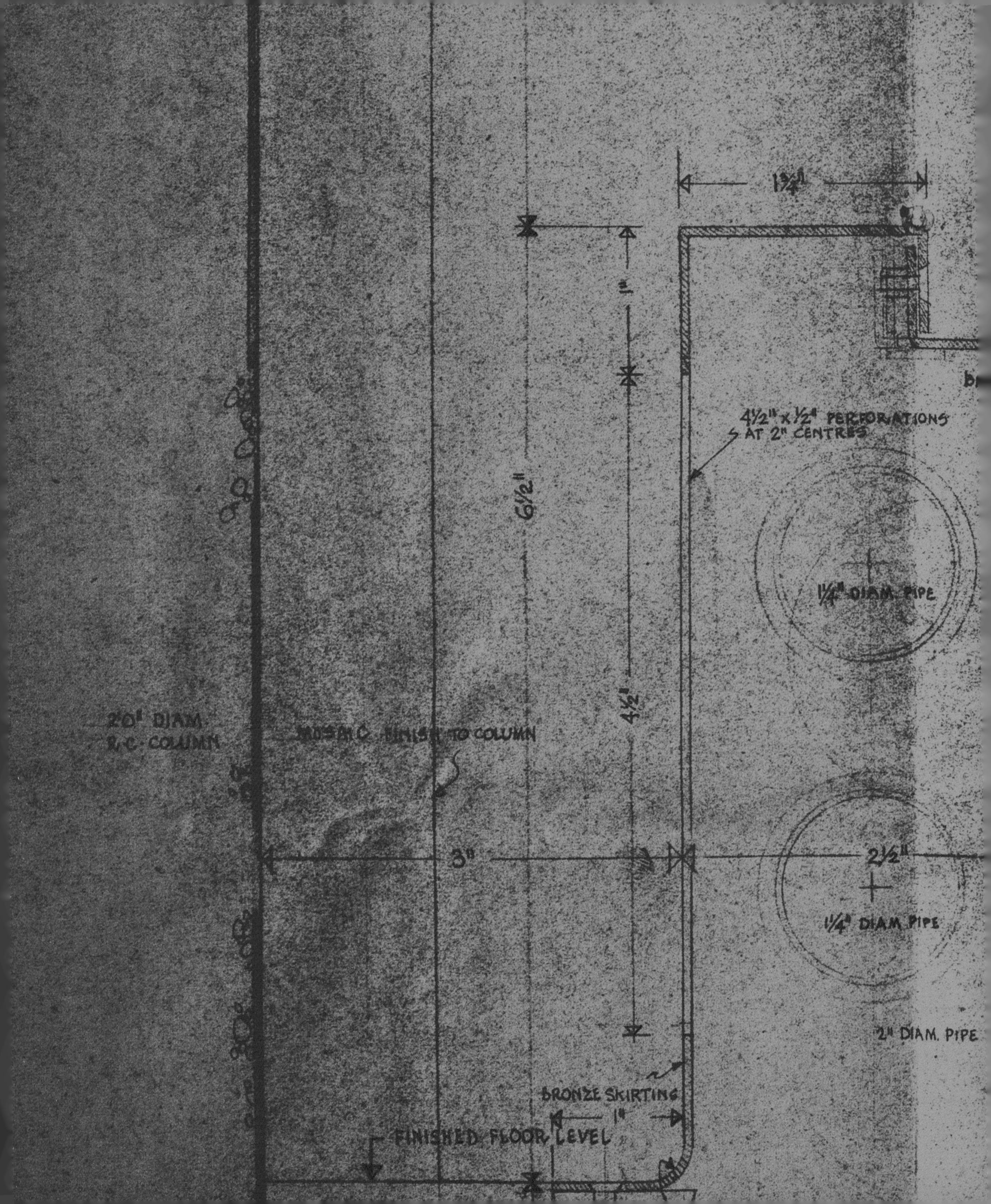
1¾"
1"
6½"
4½" x ½" PERFORATIONS
AT 2" CENTRES
1¼" DIAM. PIPE
4½"
2'0" DIAM.
R.C. COLUMN
MOSAIC FINISH TO COLUMN
3"
2½"
1¼" DIAM. PIPE
2" DIAM. PIPE
BRONZE SKIRTING
1"
FINISHED FLOOR LEVEL

Philosophy

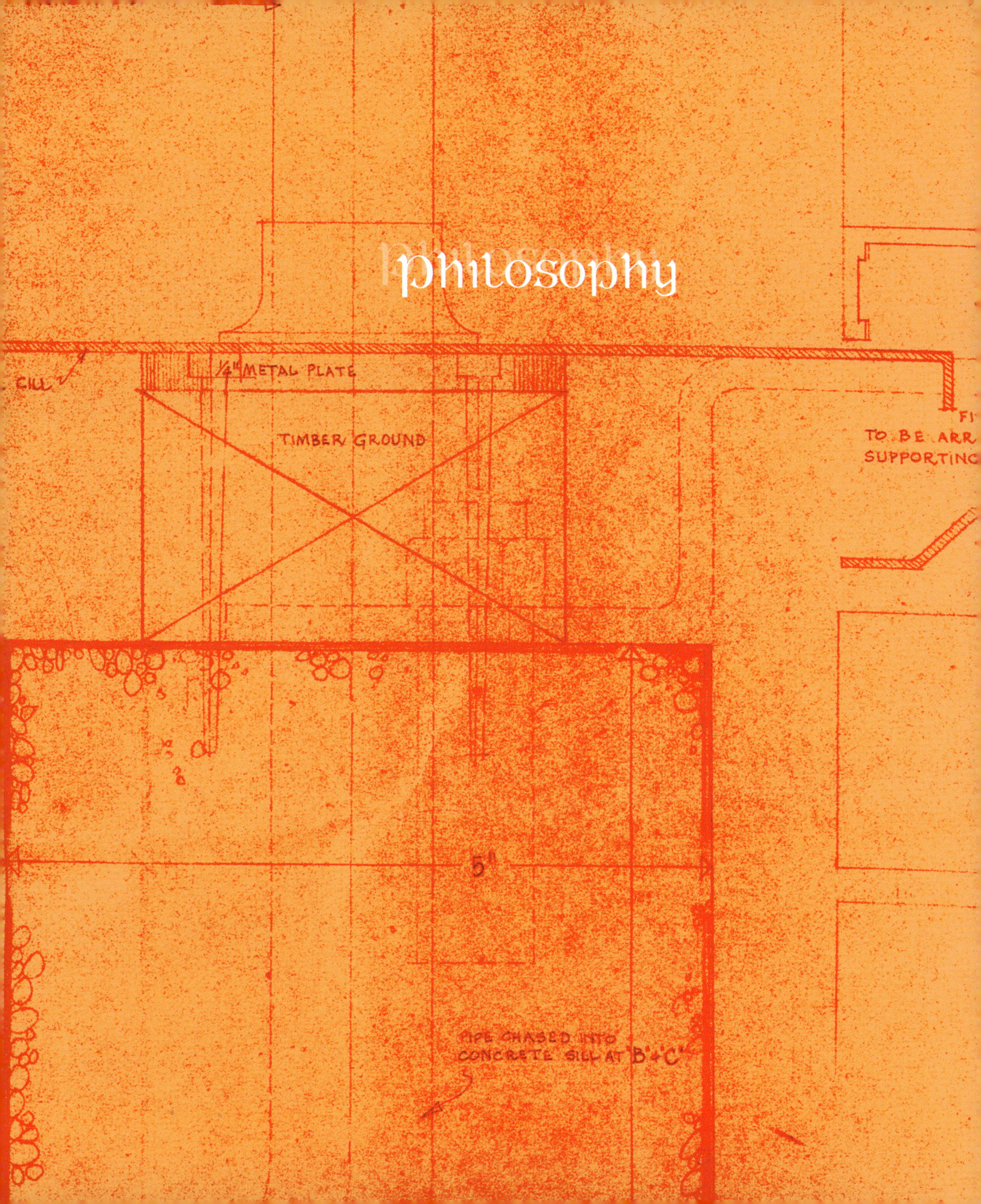
CILL
1/4" METAL PLATE
TIMBER GROUND
5"
PIPE CHASED INTO
CONCRETE SILL AT 'B' + 'C'

Philosophy

Irish society did not have to await the twentieth century to undergo the shock of modernity: disintegration and fragmentation were already part of its history so that, in a crucial but not always welcome sense, Irish culture experienced modernity before its time.

Luke Gibbons

Three Buildings – Three Irelands

If you stand on George's Quay just by Talbot Memorial Bridge on the south side of the River Liffey and look north, you glimpse three of Dublin's most important buildings.

On the left and in the foreground is the Custom House. Built over a decade from 1781 to 1791, it was commissioned by the then head of Revenue, John Beresford, who appointed James Gandon as the architect. It was to replace an older Custom House as the location where duties were collected on imported goods.

Seen today by many as the architectural jewel of the city, the Custom House was controversial in its time. Not unlike its more modern neighbour Busáras, there were disputes over its location and cost. But its fine, neoclassical design and impressive decorative features have stood the test of time.

As the centre of commercial trade moved closer to the docks during the nineteenth century, the Custom House became the headquarters of the Local Government Board, before being severely damaged by the IRA during the War of Independence in 1921. Reconstructed

during the 1920s, it has since been the home of a series of government departments, including the Department of Local Government (then the Department of Environment and today the Department of Housing, Local Government and Heritage).

Gandon's Custom House represents a very particular moment in Ireland's history. Its neoclassical style exudes the pomp and grandeur of empire. Its function placed it at the epicentre of the imperial mercantile economy. It is a building depicting Ireland as part of, indeed subject to, the British Empire.

To the right of the Custom House is the IFSC. Built 200 years after its neoclassical neighbour, it is indicative of a generic postmodern style, recognisable in the financial centres of London as much as in those of New York or Frankfurt.

The brainchild of leading Irish businessman and financier Dermot Desmond, the IFSC was a central element in the state-led redevelopment of the Docklands. Designed by architects Burke, Kennedy and Doyle, it was built from 1987 to 1997. The project benefited from both the area's designation as a Special Economic Zone and from the patronage of then Taoiseach Charles Haughey.

The building was meant to play a role in the regeneration of the traditionally working-class Sheriff Street community by providing much-needed social and affordable housing and civic amenities around the canal dock. However, it has resulted in the segregation of the area's original community from the higher-income residents of the expanding higher-density apartment developments, hotels and office blocks that stretch down to the sea.

The function of the IFSC itself is even more controversial, in that it serves as a host for hundreds of brass-plate investment vehicles that avail of the city centre's – and, indeed, the country's – low tax status. It was and remains a monument to the financialisation and liberalisation of the Irish economy from the 1990s to the present day.

Burke, Kennedy and Doyle's IFSC is also a building of empire: the late twenty-first-century empire of high finance. It represents the neoliberal Ireland of the Celtic Tiger, a soulless cosmopolitanism consistent with the desire of economic and political elites to dissolve any form of Irishness into a vacuous Europeanism, devoid of meaningful cultural or civic content.

Between and behind the Custom House of Ireland's past and the IFSC of Ireland's present stands Áras Mhic Dhiarmada and Busáras. Michael Scott's mid-century modernist masterpiece represents an Ireland that could have been. For a brief moment in the late 1940s, a modernising republicanism sought to redefine the self-image of the new state, the portion of the nation it had jurisdiction over and that state's relationship with the wider public.

As discussed in earlier chapters, much of this forward-looking nation-building project took the form of public buildings, including hospitals, schools and public utilities. However, Busáras represents an important high point in this short-lived moment, as it gathered together elements of nation building, cultural-identity formation, public-service provision and innovation in engineering and design. Taken as a whole, these elements offer us an important philosophical view of what it means to be Irish, what kind of republic we are or could be, and how the state and the institutions of government should engage with their people.

While this moment did not last long, it represents a road not travelled and one that still resonates in Ireland today. In the aftermath of the recession of 2008, the Eurozone crisis of 2012 and the COVID-19 pandemic of 2020, we are at a potential turning point in the country's history. Casting our eye back to the philosophical underpinning of the Central Bus Station offers us interesting answers to many of the questions we face today about how we respond to our present and where we may go in our collective future.

Decolonisation – A Brave New World

The three driving forces behind Áras Mhic Dhiarmada – Reynolds, Scott and Lemass – represent a particular response to post-independence nation building. Ellen Rowley talks about the allure of the 'tabula rasa' that presents itself to newly independent nations, which, in a desire to break from the culture and symbols of empire, seek to construct and articulate a new vision for themselves.[1]

3005
THE BREW

For some, this involves recreating and reviving the culture and symbols of the past, celebrating pre-colonial values and practices. For others, while resting on these indigenous foundations, it moves further, embracing the future and all the promise that comes with that brave new world.

India secured her independence in the same year that construction started on Busáras. As with Ireland, India was partitioned, with the creation of the state of Pakistan. The new fault line ran through the Punjab province, with the historic regional capital on the Pakistani side of the border. The newly installed prime minister of India, Jawaharlal Nehru, decided to commission the building of a new city on the Indian side of the border. In 1953, he invited Le Corbusier to complete the design of what was to become the Indian Punjabi capital of Chandigarh. The final design of the city is a blend of Indian tradition and European modernism. The city is recognised as a UNESCO world heritage site today.

According to historian Anthony Flint: 'Nehru sought a capital that would symbolise independent India's move to modernity, liberated from being a British colony.'[2] Flint quotes Nehru as saying, 'Let it be the first large expression of our creative genius flowering on our newly earned freedom.'[3]

Áras Mhic Dhiarmada and Busáras represents a similar moment, albeit on a smaller scale. While for Taoiseach Éamon de Valera independence from Britain meant a return to rural, Gaelic and Catholic values, for Lemass, Reynolds and Scott, independence was an opportunity not only to revive that past but to embrace the future and, literally, to construct, in the physical form of public buildings, an expression of the creative genius of the newly independent nation.

There is a sense in which this short moment represented a golden age, not just of modernist architecture in the new Free State, but of a particular type of decolonising project. It sought to address the legacy problems of empire through the construction of hospitals, schools, homes and transport infrastructure, the form and design of which was not just functional but sought to portray a very specific idea of what it meant to be Irish in the postcolonial era.

A Cosmopolitan Nationalism

According to Boyd and McLaughlin, 'Scott's buildings were used in both popular and architectural culture as a means of creating a new, progressive outwardly-turning identity.'[4] But this should not be interpreted as in any way in opposition to the project of nation building then underway in the new Free State. Rather, it constitutes a very specific articulation of the nation that is both native and international in equal measure.

Scott, Reynolds and Lemass were all committed republicans and conscious participants in the building of the new Irish nation, both socially and physically. Áras Mhic Dhiarmada and Busáras is a physical manifestation of that project. Scott actively promoted Irish talent,

skills and materials through its building, from the Cavan brick to the Connemara marble. Yet this attention to sourcing local materials did not prevent him from embracing international options when they were more appropriate. His choice of Italian glass tiles or the Danish engineering innovation of Ove Arup spoke to his being attuned to what was most suited to the overall mission of the building.

This is a nationalism that is confident enough in its own sense of self not to be threatened by the potential of new and outside influences. Rather, it welcomes these influences as complements to and enhancements of the emerging national culture. What matters is the terms on which these elements are fused, not their place of origin. Indeed, Clerkin argues that this approach is 'in the tradition of the

urlár 2
má tá gaeilge agat
labair í

urlár 4
má tá gaeilge agat
labair í

Festival of Britain buildings [and their Scandinavian influences] in attempting to marry traditions of the past with the materials and social values of the present'.[5]

This innovative feature of Scott's work was already evident in his award-winning design of the Irish Pavilion for the New York World Fair in 1939. There, Scott combined the sharp and sleek line of International Modernism in a building that, from the air, was shaped like a shamrock. Looking back, Scott remembered that the government 'Liked the idea of the building. And how [he] solved this problem of nationalism and made it modern at the same time.'[6]

Significantly, Scott's one regret with the Pavilion was the government's refusal to allow 'Éire' to be used as the building's name sign, opting for the more universally understandable 'Ireland'.[7]

Similar nods to traditional Irish culture can be seen in Scott's choice of Colm Ó Lochlainn to design the never-to-be completed signage for Áras Mhic Dhiarmada, and the small floor signs on the Department of Social Protection stairwell with the words inscribed in Celtic script: *má tá Gaeilge agat labhair í* (if you have Irish speak it). This is a nationalism that celebrates the past and local indigenous culture and language without being limited by them. It brings them on a journey into the future, expanding and reworking what it means to be Irish in the era of modernity.

While some modernists brashly followed the American avant-garde poet Ezra Pound in his demand to abandon tradition and 'make it new', others, including Scott, understood that the relationship between tradition and modernity is more nuanced. This interplay of past and future in the articulation of national identity becomes all the more salient when one reconsiders the relationship between metropole and periphery throughout the twentieth century.

It is a mistake to think about buildings such as Busáras as being part of a localised, parochial vernacular of some universalist standard first developed in London or Paris or Berlin. As Srnicek and Williams make clear, the claim to universality, particularly emerging from metropolitan Europe in the mid-twentieth century, was all about asserting the particular vernacular modernism of more powerful cultural

centres, and claiming it to be some form of universal standard over the corresponding forms in the periphery.[8] It is more useful to understand the history of modernism generally, and modernist architecture specifically, as a series of national and regional forms connected by a shared international language that is not only compatible with but enhanced by particular customs, materials and crafts whose origins are distinctly national and local.

This was understood at the time, as evidenced in John Hinde's postcards depicting images of both the traditional thatched cottage and donkey carts laden with turf in rural Ireland alongside the new, modern Ireland as represented by Collinstown Airport. Similarly, the 1956 *Ireland of the Welcomes* travel magazine combined 'a hyper real ancient Irish past ... with images of Busáras'.[9]

Áras Mhic Dhiarmada and Busáras is an Irish building and an international building without contradiction; it embodies Ireland's cultural past, present and future; it is both nationalist and cosmopolitan in equal measure, redefining what it meant to be Irish in the late 1940s and early 1950s.

Republican, Social Democratic and Populist

Writing in 1956 about Busáras, the architect Niall Montgomery described the language displayed by the building as a 'democratic republicanism'.[10] This idea that the building, in both its form and use, embodies both republican and democratic values runs to the very core of what Scott and Reynolds were trying to achieve.

As with Nehru and Le Corbusier in Chandigarh, which would 'serve people of all classes, including the very poor who were to be provided with a means to live there with dignity',[11] for Scott and his team, the central intention of Busáras was to enable all people to travel with dignity. Clerkin talks of the building's 'egalitarianism', not just in that it was about 'transport for the masses', but because it was providing ordinary people with the culture, comfort and luxury normally reserved for the wealthy.[12]

Two important principles are at work here. Rowley argues that while,

during the 1930s and early 1940s, there was a great sense of optimism among the first generation of nation builders in the Free State, there was also a growing realisation that the social problems that existed in Ireland could no longer be blamed on Britain.[13] This generation had a responsibility to ensure that as the nation was being built it would be built for all of its people.

There is a deep-seated civic republicanism at work in Busáras as government (Lemass), commerce (Reynolds) and artists (Scott *et al.*) worked together to provide the general public with a vital public service. The Central Bus Station becomes a vehicle not only for providing world-class public transport, but, in doing so, physically representing the

promise of the 1916 Proclamation to 'cherish all of the children equally'.

As Godson argues, while CIÉ and then the Department of Social Welfare had commissioned Michael Scott and his team, there is a very clear sense that for the crafters of the building the wider public was the real client.[14]

The high-quality materials, the open space and constant natural light, the beautifully crafted furniture and fittings, the wide range of planned amenities and services were all intended for the plain people of Ireland as they travelled to and from the capital to work, attend hospital, pay their respects at a funeral, visit family and friends, attend Croke Park for an All-Ireland final or go shopping. Crucially the Central Bus Station was

meant to be an open public space, the most compelling features of which were accessible to all.

It is no accident that the sixth-floor restaurant and balconies, with their spectacular views of the city, also had the most beautiful mosaics. In a similar bid to accommodate and educate Irish citizens at a time when people didn't have access to television, bus passengers and passers-by could pop down to the basement to watch the twenty-four-hour newsreel.

This was not the austere republicanism of de Valera, but a more expansive, almost social democratic republicanism, typified by the quasi-social democratic Seán Lemass.

Indeed there is a certain populism at work here, both in the building's form and function. As Clerkin argues, the curves of concrete canopy over the concourse soften the more ridged form of the building's main body. But this is more than just a nod to the populist 'style of the Festival of Britain'.[15]

The entire building exudes a democratic populism that would become more widespread in post-war, welfare-state Britain, or Germany, in which avant-garde architectural and design styles were combined with public buildings such as schools, hospitals, libraries and bus stations. This is intended to be a popular architecture, a people's building, where high culture meets everyday life, to the mutual benefit of both.

As Clerkin described it above, the bus station was to be a 'microcosm of the city', a condensed *res publica*, a commonwealth, provided by the democratically elected government, servicing the interests of the people in a manner that recognised the dignity of everyday life.

The travelling public had long agitated for a shelter from the rain, a simple utilitarian demand to make the business of travel less burdensome. Instead, Scott, Reynolds and their team wanted 'to make travel a pleasurable event rather than an inconvenience to be undergone'.[16]

This was pleasure as a public good, not a commercial product, delivered to all on an equal basis, designed to improve the quality of people's lives as they went about the most mundane or important parts of their day.

Back to George's Quay

Today, when I stand on George's Quay just by Talbot Memorial Bridge on the south side of the River Liffey and look north, I see a lot more than three buildings. I get a glimpse of what our future could look like.

If Scott and his team were designing and building Busáras today, with the same desire to use the most modern and innovative engineering techniques and materials, they would not be using concrete slab and glass. Adapting their approach to a major public building in the era of climate change would demand a completely different approach to address the challenge of embedded carbon, energy efficiency and sustainability. Instead of air conditioning and internal vacuum systems, there would be electric charging points for a green fleet of buses, and on-site solar and wind energy generation to provide the building with as much of its own renewable power as possible.

Scott would still endeavour to make the building a public space, with the best of amenities for all travellers. It would adapt to universal design to ensure that people of all abilities had equal access to all services. Maybe he would add a carbon sink urban wood on the roof as part of an expanded public restaurant.

The core philosophical principles of integrating past and present, tradition and modernity, would live on in new and exciting forms. More importantly, the building would be loudly reclaiming and proclaiming the virtue of well-designed and planned public space, a commonwealth for the twenty-first century, designed for all, open to all, enjoyed by all.

When you look around Dublin today, or indeed Ireland's other cities and towns, how many such buildings that have been built in recent decades do you see? The Carlow Visual Arts Centre, the Waterford Museum of Treasures and maybe a few others.

How many public projects have invited young architects and designers just out of college – as were Cantwell, Scott, Walker and others – and given them free creative rein, coupled with a guiding hand of experience, to produce works of real quality and durability?

We are still living in an era where public architecture is a relic of the past. Public space continues to be commercialised and privatised.

The unwillingness of government to invest in the public realm leaves important public amenities – like the Writers' Quarter in Parnell Square – unrealised or, worse still, at the mercy of private finance.

Today, a contemporary Michael Scott would still be railing against a contemporary Dan O'Donovan, demanding the best materials and the most beautiful design for the public. The tragedy today is the scarcity of ministers and public servants with the political will and nation-building vision of Lemass or Reynolds, dedicated to ensuring that at least some of the architect's vision would be realised.

It doesn't matter whether you think Áras Mhic Dhiarmada and Busáras an ugly building, or dated, or simply uninteresting. What matters are the ideas that drove it and, for this writer at least, continue to keep it alive today.

Those ideas are as relevant in the twenty-first century as they were in the 1940s and 1950s. In our politics, our culture and our public realm, we need to reclaim the values of cosmopolitan nationalism, civic republicanism, social democracy and democratic populism that inspired Lemass, Reynolds and Scott. We need to do this in order to provide services, amenities and cultural artefacts that are respectful of the past, excited about the future, confident in their Irishness, embracing of international trends and ideas, democratic in design and purpose and, most importantly, egalitarian in form, function and use.

Áras Mhic Dhiarmada and Busáras have a lot to teach us. Respecting the building is not about cultivating a nostalgia for a past style, which rightly belongs in our architectural history, another layer to be cherished in the fabric of our capital city. Rather, it is about learning from that past, while always looking to create a new and exciting future. The question today is whether we have the capacity and willingness to learn from that short but exciting period that produced one of the most interesting buildings of the twentieth century, Michael Scott's Busáras.

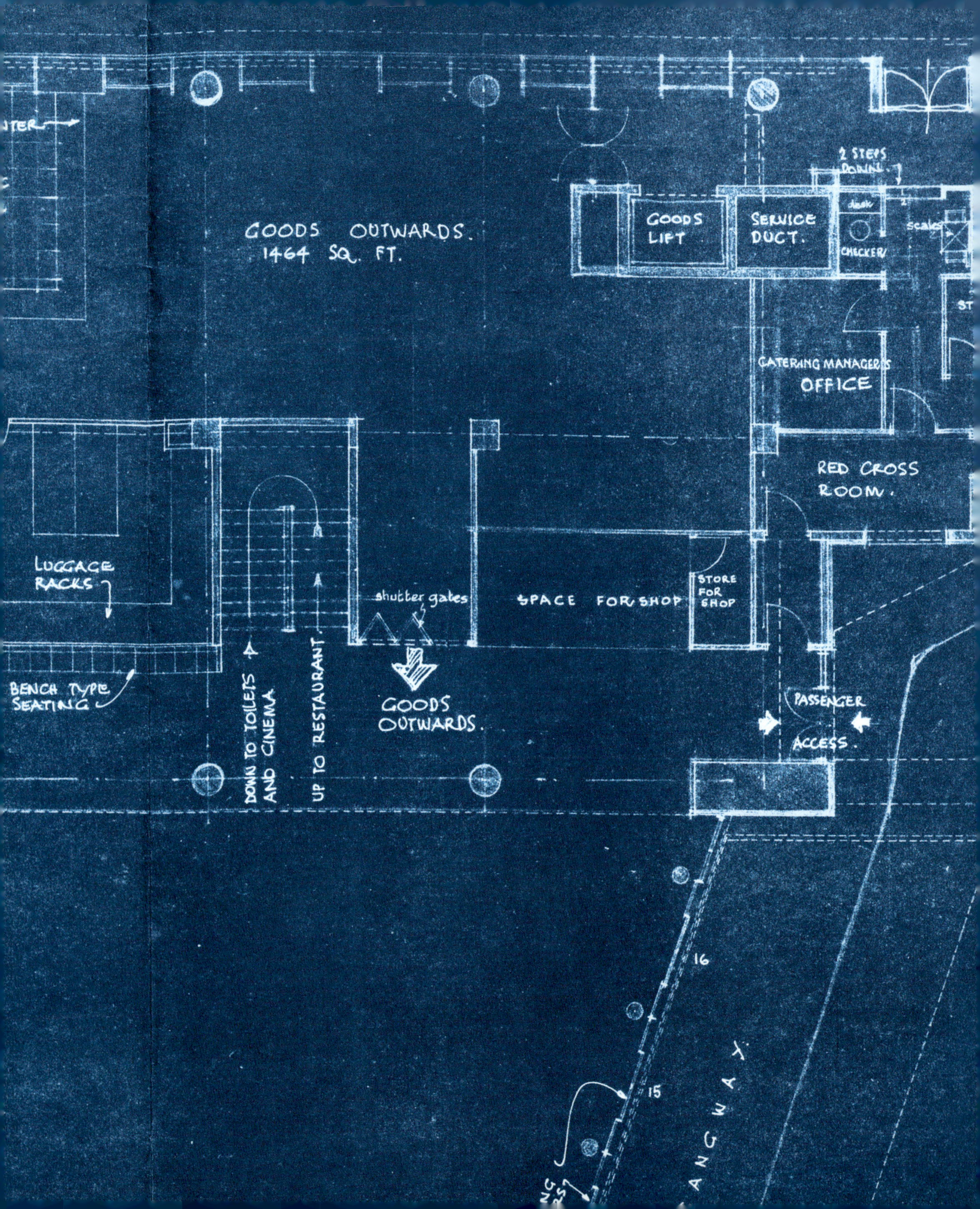

GOODS OUTWARDS.
1464 SQ. FT.
GOODS LIFT
SERVICE DUCT.
2 STEPS DOWN
desk
CHECKER
scales
CATERING MANAGER'S OFFICE
RED CROSS ROOM.
LUGGAGE RACKS
shutter gates
SPACE FOR SHOP
STORE FOR SHOP
BENCH TYPE SEATING
DOWN TO TOILETS AND CINEMA
UP TO RESTAURANT
GOODS OUTWARDS.
PASSENGER ACCESS.
16
15

Departure

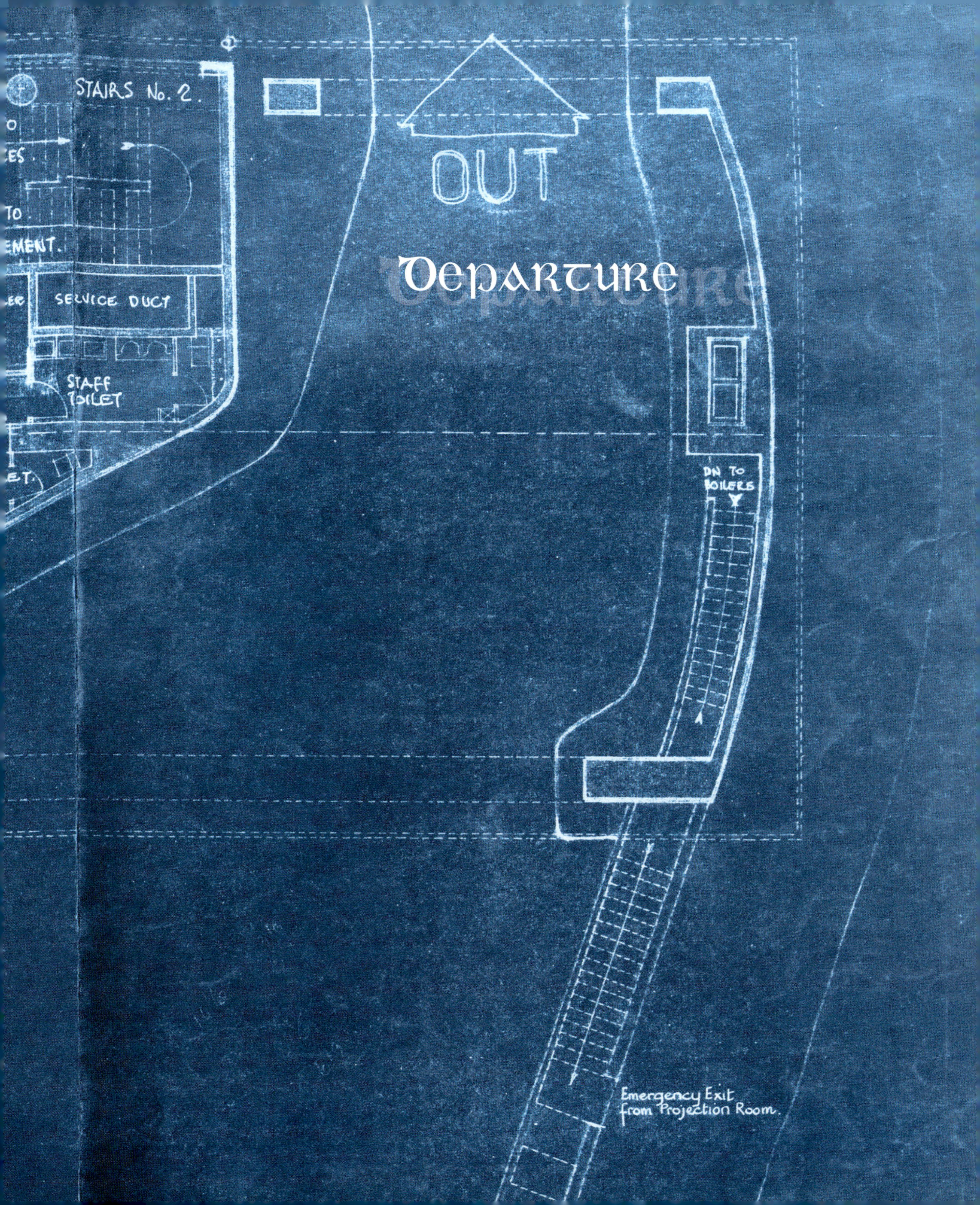
STAIRS No. 2
OUT
SERVICE DUCT
STAFF TOILET
DN TO BOILERS
Emergency Exit from Projection Room.

BUS EIREANN
ENTRANCE
Bus Éireann

Departure

Áras Mhic Dhiarmada and Busáras have been open and operational for sixty-eight years. Parts of the building, including the foundations and concrete shell, are more than seventy years old. Despite its age, both the bus station and the Department of Social Protection headquarters continue to function in the same way as when they opened. The building has, without doubt, stood the test of time.

The management and maintenance of such an old building require a significant amount of ongoing expenditure to clean, repair and insure. Both Bus Éireann and the Department of Social Protection have had to constantly adapt to ensure the continued functioning of the building.

While the government's Social Insurance Fund is the owner of the building, Bus Éireann has a 200-year lease on the basement, concourse and mezzanine floor at a peppercorn rent.

Unfortunately, constrained finances have meant that, despite its good structural condition, the building is not without its problems. Leaks in the basement and problems with the heating and air conditioning in the Department's offices are all symptoms of a building in need of greater attention.

While an enhanced cleaning regime in both its public and external areas has improved the general look of the building, Busáras is not treated in the same manner as older buildings of significant architectural merit, such as the Custom House, General Post Office or City Hall. There is little external lighting to help showcase the building at night, and the overall cleanliness of the external façades leaves much to be desired.

03
Dublin Express
Translink
Goldline
TAKE IT EASY
FAN GLAN
KEEP
CLEAR

Thankfully, both the Department of Social Protection and Bus Éireann have advanced plans for the restoration and modernisation of the building. However, any works will ultimately be dependent on funding approval from government. At the time of writing, the impact of COVID-19 on the Social Insurance Fund has put the Department of Social Protection's plans on hold.

In August of this year, the secretary general of the Department of Social Protection, John McKeon, outlined what he believes should happen to the building. Following discussions with the Office of Public Works and State Architect Ciarán O'Connor, a series of options for the refurbishment and modernisation of Áras Mhic Dhiarmada and Busáras were scoped.

In addition to restoring and repairing the building and its iconic features, such as the terrazzo floors and mosaic pillars and murals, there is also a lot of upgrading required. This would include new heating, air conditioning and fire-safety measures. Initial costs put the scale of the work anywhere between €60 million and €100 million. The volume of work would also require staff to decant to temporary accommodation.

McKeon not only believes that this work should be done but argues that, as the building is an asset of the Social Insurance Fund, it makes sense to restore and upgrade it. Importantly, the secretary general is keen that, if and when any refurbishment takes place, it should be part of the wider regeneration of the north-east inner city. Consistent with the mission of the Department, McKeon would like to see local employment and apprenticeships form part of any programme.

Despite only having worked in the building for three years, McKeon has grown very attached to it. He describes it as an 'architectural pearl' and part of 'the city's heritage that should be maintained'. He argues that the building 'compares well' with any of the surrounding important buildings, such as the Custom House, and that he is both 'proud of it' and very 'defensive of it'.[1]

Before the onset of the pandemic, McKeon says the plans for refurbishment were quite advanced, but the financial impact of the pandemic on the Social Insurance Fund will obviously have a bearing on whether they are revived.

Across the concourse in Busáras, Bus Éireann Regional Manager for the East Adrian O'Loughlin has responsibility for managing the bus station. He has worked there for twenty-one years, starting in the ticket office, and the building is now also his office.

Back in 2015, Bus Éireann secured planning permission for the development of office space on the mezzanine floor as well as a series of upgrades to the disability access and fire-safety aspects of the building. The planning permission was subsequently extended until April 2026. However, following a review of all of Bus Éireann's facilities and properties, a series of possible revisions of the initial plans has been considered as part of a ten-year plan to upgrade bus services.

At the centre of this plan is a desire to increase the number of staff located in the building, improve the working environment and facilities for employees, and enhance the customer experience, with a particular focus on disability access.

The bus company would like to see the number of staff working in the building increase from twenty to ninety, in addition to providing better working and recreational facilities for all staff. Importantly, it wants to fully restore the theatre space in the basement to provide a 140-seat training and meeting facility. As with the rest of the building, the basement will need fire-safety and accessibility upgrades, including the installation of a lift.

There are no estimated costings available yet, as the revised planning permission has yet to be secured. Once that has taken place, Bus Éireann will then have to seek approval for the finances with their parent body, CIÉ, and the National Transport Authority, in order to commence the work.

If Busáras had been built in the eighteenth or nineteenth century, it is highly likely that it would be in better condition, particularly on the outside, than it is today. However, being a modernist relic of the twentieth century, it does not fit into everyone's understanding of a heritage building, worthy of being protected and promoted.

Yet can you imagine the impact on the approach from either Middle Abbey Street or Amiens Street if the building was cleaned, restored and properly lit at night, displaying its crisp, clean, modernist architecture;

the wonderful, warm mosaics and pillars; and the bronze and copper metalwork?

Pre-COVID-19, 131 arrivals and 170 departures passed through Busáras every single day, carrying in excess of 1,500 passengers. Next door, hundreds of civil servants kept the central hub of the Department of Social Protection in motion, providing hundreds of thousands of households with a variety of supports. Beyond that, thousands of people pass the building every single day on foot, by bicycle, Luas, bus and train.

While being interviewed for this book, entertainer and publican Rory O'Neill (aka Panti Bliss) expressed longing for a better viewing point for the building, to allow the general public to better appreciate it. He proposed a solution of removing the iron railings that surround the Custom House, so as to transform the Department of Housing green into a public garden where people can sit and take in the many wonderful features of Áras Mhic Dhiarmada and Busáras.

If we are to change the minds of ambivalent or indeed hostile passengers and passers-by about this 'architectural pearl', we will have to break down the decades of barriers erected by the building's design, location and inaccessibility. Greater use of the building for public events, and the restoration of the Eblana Theatre, would assist greatly, as would more public access to tours of and events on the sixth-floor restaurant and balcony.

Having spoken at length to the two principal custodians of the building, Adrian O'Loughlin of Bus Éireann and John McKeon of the Department of Social Protection, I have no doubt of their desire to see the building shine for staff and public alike. Now all we have to do is convince those who control the purse strings, in government, in CIÉ and in the National Transport Authority, of the merits of the restoration.

Endnotes

Arrival

1 Ellen Rowley (ed.), *More Than Concrete Blocks: Dublin City's Twentieth-Century Buildings and Their Stories, Volume 2: 1940–72* (Dublin: Four Courts Press, 2018), p. 185.

History

1 Terence Brown, *Ireland: A Social and Cultural History, 1922 to the Present* (Ithaca, NY: Fontana Press, 1985), p. 174.
2 Brendan Lynch, *Prodigals and Geniuses: The Writers and Artists of Dublin's Baggotonia* (Dublin: The Liffey Press, 2011).
3 Luke Gibbons, *Transformations in Irish Culture* (Cork: Cork University Press, 1996), pp. 75, 78, 102.
4 Enrique Juncosa and Christina Kennedy (eds), *The Moderns: The Arts in Ireland from the 1990s to the 1970s* (Dublin: Irish Museum of Modern Art, 2011), p. 97.
5 Paul Clerkin, 'Michael Scott's Busáras Building, Dublin 1944–1953' (unpublished MA thesis, 1996), p. 26.
6 Ibid.
7 Interview with the author, December 2020.
8 Shaun Boylan, 'Reynolds, Augustus Percival Harald' in James McGuire and James Quinn (eds), *Dictionary of Irish Biography* (Cambridge: Cambridge University Press, 2020).
9 Micheal Ó Riain, 'Always under pressure, Córas Iompair Éireann and Irish Public Transport' in *Irish Quarterly Review*, Vol. 86, No. 341 (Spring 1997), p. 63.
10 Ibid.
11 Ibid.
12 John O'Regan and Nicola Dearey (eds), *Michael Scott, Architect: In (Casual) Conversation with Dorothy Walker* (Kinsale: Gandon Editions, 1995), p. 53.
13 Ibid., p. 71.
14 Paul Larmour, *Free State Architecture: Modern Movement Architecture in Ireland, 1922–1949* (Kinsale: Gandon Editions, 2009), p. 62.
15 Clerkin (1996), p. 134.
16 Ibid.
17 Ibid., p. 133.
18 Ciarán O'Connor, 'Busáras/City Planning: The Custom House and the Busáras Project' (n.d., unpublished paper), p. 2.
19 Ibid.
20 Ibid., p. 3.
21 Ibid.
22 Ibid.
23 Paul Clerkin, 'Fifty Years of Busáras' in *History Ireland*, vol. 11, issue 2 (Summer 2003), p. 39.
24 O'Connor (n.d.), p. 5.
25 Clerkin (1996), p. 52.
26 Ibid.
27 Ibid.
28 Ibid., p. 53.
29 Ibid., p. 54.
30 Ibid.
31 *The Irish Times*, 5 May 1950.
32 Clerkin (1996), p. 58.
33 *The Irish Times*, 22 December 1950.
34 Clerkin (1996), p. 63.
35 Ibid., p. 75.
36 Personal correspondence of Scott, 1952, held in the Irish Architectural Archive, Dublin.
37 Personal correspondence of O'Donovan, 1952, held in the Irish Architectural Archive, Dublin.
38 Ibid.
39 O'Connor (n.d.), p. 11.
40 'Dublin's Newest Building, the Store Street C.I.E. Bus Station and Government Offices', *Irish Builder and Engineer*, 7 November 1953.
41 O'Regan and Deary (1995), p. 158.
42 John O'Regan (ed.), *Michael Scott, 1905–1989* (Kinsale: Gandon Books, 1993), p. 6.
43 'Buzzin for Busáras', www.rabble.ie, 9 November 2017.

Architecture

1 O'Regan and Dearey (1995), p. 68.
2 Quote from *Build* magazine, 1976, cited in Clerkin (1996).
3 Walter Gropius, *The New Architecture and the Bauhaus*, trans. P. Morton Shand (London: Faber & Faber, 1965), p. 24.
4 Ibid., pp. 28–9.
5 Ibid., p. 33.
6 Ibid., p. 40.
7 Ibid., p. 52.
8 Ibid., pp. 57, 62.
9 Ibid., p. 66.
10 Ibid., pp. 79–80.
11 Ibid., p. 85.
12 Ibid., p. 92.
13 Ibid., p. 112.
14 Fiona MacCarthy, *Walter Gropius: Visionary Founder of the Bauhaus* (London: Faber & Faber, 2019), p. 48.
15 Ibid., p. 121.
16 Gropius (1965), p. 112.
17 Larmour (2009), pp. 18–21.
18 Ibid., p. 97.
19 Ibid.
20 Clerkin (1996), p. 40.
21 Interview with Clerkin, 1996.
22 Ibid.
23 Ibid.

24 *Irish Builder and Engineer*, 7 November 1953.
25 Ibid.
26 Interview with the author, December 2020.
27 *Irish Builder and Engineer*, 7 November 1953.
28 Ibid.
29 Ibid.
30 Ibid.
31 Ibid.
32 Clerkin (1996), p. 89.
33 Larmour (2009), p. 88.
34 Ibid.
35 Rowley (2018), p. 185.
36 Ibid.
37 Clerkin (1996), p. 71.
38 Ibid.
39 Interview with the author, December 2020.
40 Ibid.
41 Interview with the author, December 2020.
42 Ibid.
43 Ibid.
44 Interview with the author, December 2020.
45 Ibid.

Design

1 Clerkin (1996), p. 109.
2 Ibid.
3 Interview with the author, December 2020.
4 MacCarthy (2019), p. 128.
5 Clerkin (1996), p. 135.
6 Barry Turner, *Beacon for Change: How the 1951 Festival of Britain Shaped the Modern Age* (London: Aurum Press Ltd, 2011), p. 1.
7 Ibid., p. 4.
8 Ibid., p. 30.
9 Ibid.
10 Interview with the author, December 2020.
11 Ibid.
12 Interview with the author, December 2020.
13 Interviews with the author, December 2020.
14 Clerkin (1996), p. 97.
15 Ibid., p. 141.
16 Basil Clancy, *Áras Mhic Dhiarmada: Offices for the Department of Social Welfare and a Bus Station for Córas Iompair Éireann at Store Street, Dublin* (Dublin: self-published, 1954).
17 Interview with the author, 2020.
18 Clerkin (1996), p. 34.
19 Ibid., p. 97.
20 Interview with the author, December 2020.
21 Ibid.
22 Ibid.

Philosophy

1 Ellen Rowley interview with the author, December 2020.
2 Anthony Flint, *Modern Man: The Life of Le Corbusier, Architect of Tomorrow* (Boston, MA: New Harvest/ Haughton Mifflin Harcourt, 2014), p. 145.
3 Ibid.
4 GaryA. Boyd and John McLaughlin (eds), *Infra Éireann: Infrastructure and the Architectures of Modernity 1916–2016* (London: Routledge, 2015).
5 Clerkin (1996), p. 17.
6 O'Regan and Dearey (1995), p. 81.
7 Ibid.
8 Nick Srnicek and Alex Williams, *Inventing the Future: Postcapitalism and a World without Work* (New York: Verso, 2016).
9 Luke Gibbons, *Transformations in Irish Culture* (Cork: Cork University Press, 1996).
10 Quoted in Rowley (2018), p. 187.
11 Flint (2014), p. 150.
12 Clerkin (1996), p. 97.
13 Interview with the author, December 2020.
14 Interview with the author, December 2020.
15 Ibid.
16 Clerkin (1996), p. 18.

Departure

1 Interview with the author, August 2021.

Bibliography

Arnold, Bruce, *Maine Jellett and the Modern Movement in Ireland* (New Haven, CT: Yale University Press, 1991).

Boyd, Gary A. and John McLaughlin, *Infra Éireann: Infra-structure and the Architectures of Modernity in Ireland 1916–2016* (London: Routledge, 2015).

Boylan, Shaun, 'Reynolds, Augustus Percival Harald' in James McGuire and James Quinn (eds), *Dictionary of Irish Biography* (Cambridge: Cambridge University Press, 2020).

Brown, Terence, *Ireland: A Social and Cultural History 1922–1985* (New York: Fontana Press, 1985).

Burke, David, *The Lawn Road Flats: Spies, Writers and Artists* (Woodbridge: The Boydell Press, 2014).

Castle, Gregory and Patrick Bixby (eds), *A History of Irish Modernism* (Cambridge: Cambridge University Press, 2019).

Clancy, Basil, *Áras Mhic Dhiarmada: Offices for the Department of Social Welfare and a Bus Station for Córas Iompair Éireann at Store Street, Dublin* (self-published, 1954).

Clerkin, Paul, 'Michael Scott's Busáras Building, Dublin 1944–1953' (unpublished MA thesis, NCAD, 1996).

Clerkin, Paul, 'Fifty Years of Busáras' in *History Ireland*, vol. 11, issue 2 (Summer 2003).

Crow, Thomas, *The Hidden Mod in Modern Art: London 1957–1969* (New Haven, CT: Yale University Press, 2020).

Curtis, William J.R., *Modern Architecture Since 1900* (London: Phaidon, 1996).

Darwent, Charles, *Josef Albers: Life and Work* (London: Thames and Hudson, 2018).

Daybelge, Leyla and Magnus Englund, *Isokon and the Bauhaus in Britain* (London: Batsford, 2019).

Devery, Catríona, 'Buzzin for Busaras', rabble.ie (2017).

Droste, Magdalena, *Bauhaus 1919–1933* (Cologne: Taschen, 2002).

'Dublin's Newest Building, the Store Street C.I.E. Bus Station and Government Offices', *Irish Builder and Engineer*, 7 November 1953.

Flint, Anthony, *Modern Man: The Life of Le Corbusier, Architect of Tomorrow* (Boston, MA: New Harvest/Haughton Mifflin Harcourt, 2014).

Gibbons, Luke, *Transformations in Irish Culture* (Cork: Cork University Press, 1996).

Gropius, Walter, *The New Architecture and the Bauhaus*, trans. P. Morton Shand (London: Faber & Faber, 1965).

Hatherley, Owen, *Red Metropolis: Socialism and the Government of London* (London: Repeater Books, 2020).

Juncosa, Enrique and Christina Kennedy (eds), *The Moderns: The Arts in Ireland from the 1990s to the 1970s* (Dublin: Irish Museum of Modern Art, 2011).

Kennedy, Róisín, *Art and the Nation State: The Reception of Modern Art in Ireland* (Liverpool: Liverpool University Press, 2021).

Larmour, Paul, *Free State Architecture: Modern Movement Architecture in Ireland 1922–1949* (Kinsale: Gandon Editions, 2009).

Le Corbusier, *Towards a New Architecture* (Eastford, CT: Martino Publishing, 2014).

Lynch, Brendan, *Prodigals and Geniuses: The Writers and Artists of Dublin's Baggotonia* (Dublin: The Liffey Press, 2011).

MacCarthy, Fiona, *Walter Gropius: Visionary Founder of the Bauhaus* (London: Faber and Faber, 2019).

Maclean, Caroline, *Circles & Squares: The Lives & Art of the Hampstead Modernists* (London: Bloomsbury, 2021).

O'Connor, Ciarán, 'Busáras/City Planning: The Custom House and the Busáras Project' (n.d., unpublished paper).

O'Connor, Éimear (ed.), *Seán Keating in Context: Responses to Culture and Politics in Post-Civil War Ireland* (Bray: Carysfort Press, 2009).

O'Regan, John (ed.), *Michael Scott, 1905–1989* (Dublin: Gandon Editions, 1993).

O'Regan, John (ed.), *Scott Tallon Walker, Architects: 100 Buildings and Projects, 1960–2005* (Kinsale: Gandon Editions, 2006).

O'Regan, John and Nicola Dearey (eds), *Michael Scott, Architect: In (Casual) Conversation with Dorothy Walker* (Kinsale: Gandon Editions, 1995).

Ó Riain, Micheal, 'Always under pressure, Córas Iompair Éireann and Irish Public Transport' in *Irish Quarterly Review*, Vol. 86, No. 341 (Spring 1997).

Rowley, Ellen (ed.), *More Than Concrete Blocks: Dublin City's Twentieth-Century Buildings and Their Stories, Volume 2: 1940–72* (Dublin: Four Courts Press, 2018).

Rowley, Ellen, *Housing, Architecture and the Edge Condition: Dublin Is Building 1935–1975* (London: Routledge, 2019).

Turner, Barry, *Beacon for Change: How the 1951 Festival of Britain Shaped the Modern Age* (London: Aurum Press, 2011).

Van Doesburg, Theo, *Principles of Neo-Plastic Art* (Zurich: Lars Müller Publishers, 2020).

List of Illustrations

All photographs by Mal McCann unless otherwise stated.

pp. 114–15: Original architectural drawing of basement plan including cinema (Irish Architectural Archive).
p. 116: Eblana theatre seating, Busáras basement.
p. 117: (clockwise) Busáras basement corridor to Eblana theatre; theatre stage; empty mineral bottles and flyers from the final 1995 performance.
p. 118: Bicycle storage sign and racks, Áras Mhic Dhiarmada basement.
p. 119: Bicycle ramp from basement to street level, Busáras.
pp. 120–1: Original service drawings for soil waste and surface water drains.
p. 124: Áras Mhic Dhiarmada terrazzo tile stairwell.
p. 126: Brass plug socket in Busáras concourse; brass air vent in Áras Mhic Dhiarmada reception.
pp. 128–9: (l–r) furniture and artwork in Áras Mhic Dhiarmada ministerial office.
p. 130: Handrail in Busáras mezzanine restaurant.
p. 132: Connemara marble on sixth floor of Áras Mhic Dhiarmada stairwell.
pp. 135–7: Gold mosaic tile skylights and red mosaic tile pillars in sixth-floor canteen, Áras Mhic Dhiarmada.
pp. 138–9: Mosaic tile diamond mural, Áras Mhic Dhiarmada roof-top canopy.
pp. 140–1: Mosaic tile leaf murals on Áras Mhic Dhiarmada sixth-floor balcony.
pp. 142–3: Original architectural drawing of Áras Mhic Dhiarmada sixth-floor restaurant and balcony (Irish Architectural Archive).
pp. 144–5: Details of iron railings on third-floor balcony, Áras Mhic Dhiarmada.
pp. 146–7: Details of fixtures and fittings, Áras Mhic Dhiarmada and Busáras offices.
pp. 148–9: Wood panel heating vent system, Áras Mhic Dhiarmada ministerial office.
p. 150: Mosaic tile walls at Busáras concourse stairwell to basement toilets and theatre.
p. 152: (clockwise) Original design drawing of ceiling light fixtures for basement cinema (Irish Architectural Archive); lampshade in basement; original ceiling light fixture in cinema.
p. 153: Stairs to and seating in Eblana Theatre.
pp. 154–5: Bronze doors and handles on Áras Mhic Dhiarmada balcony doors.
pp. 156–7: Passengers waiting in Busáras concourse.
p. 158: Busáras control tower with blue mosaic tile mural.
p. 160: Adrian O'Loughlin.
p. 162: Rhonda Byrne.
p. 164: Plaque for former Busáras employee Aidan Egan.
p. 165: Passengers in Busáras concourse.
p. 167: Arturas Danaitis.
p. 168: Fixtures and fittings from various floors in Áras Mhic Dhiarmada and Busáras.
p. 170: Aisling Clarke.
p. 173: Greg Simons.
p. 174: Switches, vents, doors and signs from Áras Mhic Dhiarmada basement.
p. 177: Mary Cullina.
p. 178: Padraig Murray.
p. 181: Eblana theatre stage, Busáras basement.
p. 183: Rory O'Neill.
p. 184: Busáras concourse.
p. 188: View of the Custom House, Busáras and IFSC from George's Quay.
p. 190: View of the IFSC from Áras Mhic Dhiarmada roof.
p. 193: View of Áras Mhic Dhiarmada from Amiens Street.
p. 194: View of Áras Mhic Dhiarmada west façade from Store Street.
p. 196: Séan Mac Diarmada panel in Áras Mhic Dhiarmada reception.
p. 197: Bus passenger in Busáras concourse.
p. 198: Floor numbers in Áras Mhic Dhiarmada stairwell.
p. 200: View of Áras Mhic Dhiarmada roof from Amiens Street.
p. 202: View of Irish Life Mall and Abbey Street from Áras Mhic Dhiarmada roof.
p. 203: View of Áras Mhic Dhiarmada west block roof.
p. 204: View of Dublin city from Áras Mhic Dhiarmada west balcony.
p. 206: View of the Custom House and Liberty Hall from George's Quay.
p. 210: Busáras Store Street entrance at night.
p. 212: Bus gate No. 3, Busáras concourse.

Index **Numbers in bold indicate images**

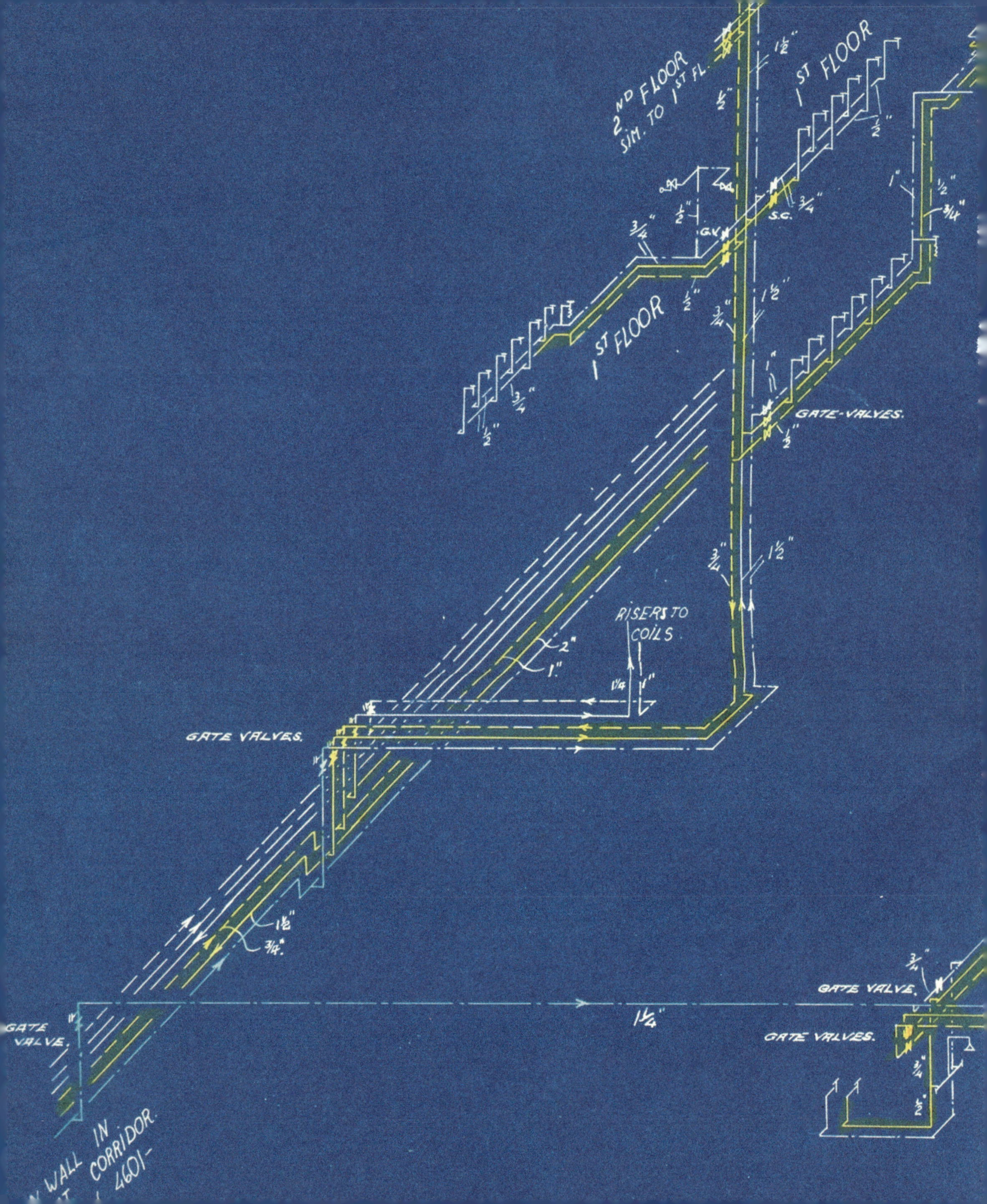

2ND FLOOR SIM. TO 1ST FL.
1ST FLOOR
1ST FLOOR
G.V.
S.C.
GATE-VALVES.
RISERS TO COILS
GATE VALVES.
GATE VALVE.
GATE VALVE.
GATE VALVES.
WALL IN CORRIDOR
4601-